Shrinking-Population
Economics

Lessons from Japan

The LTCB International Library Trust

The LTCB (Long-Term Credit Bank of Japan) International Library Trust, established in July 2000, is the successor to the LTCB International Library Foundation. It carries on the mission that the foundation's founders articulated as follows:

> The world is moving steadily toward a borderless economy and deepening international interdependence. Amid economic globalization, Japan is developing ever-closer ties with nations worldwide through trade, through investment, and through manufacturing and other localized business operations.
>
> Japan's global activity is drawing attention to its political, economic, and social systems and to the concepts and values that underlie those systems. But the supply of translations of Japanese books about those and other Japan-related subjects has not kept pace with demand.
>
> The shortage of foreign-language translations of Japanese books about Japanese subjects is attributable largely to the high cost of translating and publishing. To address that issue, the LTCB International Library Foundation funds the translation and the distribution of selected Japanese works about Japan's politics, economy, society, and culture.

International House of Japan, Inc., manages the publishing activities of the LTCB International Library Trust, and Chuo Mitsui Trust and Banking Company, Ltd., manages the trust's financial assets.

LTCB International Library Trust/International House of Japan

Shrinking-Population Economics

Lessons from Japan

Matsutani Akihiko

Professor,
National Graduate Institute for Policy Studies

Translated by
Brian Miller

Transliteration of names

The romanization of Japanese names in this book is in accordance with the Hepburn system. Surnames precede first names in accordance with Japanese custom.

This book was originally published in 2004 by Nihon Keizai Shimbun, Inc., as *Jinko Gensho Keizai no Atarashii Koshiki*. International House of Japan retains the English-language translation rights under contract with Matsutani Akihiko and through the courtesy of Nihon Keizai Shimbun.

First English edition published March 2006 by International House of Japan
11-16, Roppongi 5-chōme, Minato-ku, Tokyo 106-0032, Japan
Tel: +81-3-3470-9059   Fax: +81-3-3470-3170
E-mail: ihj@i-house.or.jp

Printed in Japan
ISBN 4-924971-18-9

CONTENTS

CHAPTER I

All at Once: The Coming Post-Max World

CHAPTER II

Expansion Becomes Shrinkage: Wrenching Change in the Business Environment

CHAPTER III

Sharing the Wealth: Reducing Regional Disparity in Economic Vitality

CHAPTER IV

Smaller Government: Rethinking Public Services

CHAPTER V

A New Social Perspective on Abundance: Focusing on Quality of Life

CHAPTER VI

A Guide Map for the Shrinking-Population Economy

FIGURES

CHAPTER I

CHAPTER II

CHAPTER III

CHAPTER IV

CHAPTER V

CHAPTER VI

Author's Introduction to the
Original (2004) Edition

Flash forward to New Year's Eve 2015. Corporate sales in Japan declined again this year for the nth year in a row (most people have stopped counting). The phrase "economic shrinkage rate" has long since replaced "economic growth rate" as standard parlance in Japanese newspapers. Most companies remain soundly profitable, however, and no one regards the economy as being in decline.

Corporate managements have finally come to terms with Japan's shrinking-population economy. When the young portion of the nation's workforce began shrinking conspicuously in the mid-1970s, industry did the wrong thing. Companies invested massively in automation to keep sales growing. Industry did the wrong thing again at the turn of the century and for a few years later. Companies lowered wage and salary levels in a vain attempt to maintain profitability. Managements finally learned, however, that a shrinking workforce mandates shrinkage in the scale of corporate operations. They finally grasped the right way—the only way—to remain viable in a shrinking-population economy: Concentrate on raising the value-added portion of sales, not on increasing gross sales volume.

Equally profound has been the change in patterns of personal behavior. Working Japanese traditionally answered the question "What do you do?" by citing their employer: "I work for [Toyota, Sony, etc.]." In 2015, they commonly respond—like their American and European counterparts—by citing their job: "I [sell cars, design computer games, etc]." Japanese have begun to value time with their families and with friends more than their time at work. Some people continue to labor away into the night at the workplace. But lots of Japanese are enjoying personal pursuits not just on weekends and holidays but even on weekdays.

Lifetime employment and seniority-based compensation fortified the competitiveness of Japanese companies in the latter half of the 20th century. They restrained overall wage costs by keeping young workers' compensation artificially low. The traditional employment system exercised the opposite effect on wage costs, however, when the workforce began to age rapidly. That forced a fin de siècle shedding of middle-aged and older workers. And in the early years of the new century, numerous Japanese companies began shifting to performance-based compensation.

Companies ceased being sanctuaries where Japanese could count on lifetime security. On the other hand, people discovered a new and exhilarating freedom. Seniority-based compensation locked people into their jobs, since seniority was not transferable. The collapse of lifetime employment and seniority-based compensation has given people unprecedented freedom to choose and change employers and even, sometimes, to choose not to work at all.

In 2015, the relationship between the individual and society has changed in ways that mirror the changes in employee-employer relations. The aging of society has forced reductions in benefits in Japan's pension system and in its national health-insurance program, and it has obliged the national and local governments to curtail public services. People need to take responsibility for providing for their needs during their working lives and in retirement. They need to manage their consumption and their savings, their work and their leisure in accordance with careful personal planning.

The preceding scenario is entirely possible—even likely. It reflects the economic implications of ongoing demographic aging and impending population shrinkage. Japan's population began aging rapidly in the 1960s. By the outset of the 21st century, the over-65 percentage of the population was larger in Japan than in any other large industrialized nation, and over the next three decades Japan's demographic profile will become increasingly and uniquely aged. The Japanese population will shrink over that period more than any other except Germany's.

Socioeconomic projections and related policy making in Japan need to begin with the understanding that population shrinkage and aging are unavoidable and, as a result, that economic shrinkage is also unavoidable. Japan's demographic trends naturally raise concerns about the outlook for the nation's economic and social health. A chorus of pundits is calling for Japan to reinforce its economic vitality by promoting child-bearing and by encouraging an influx of foreign labor. Even a pronounced rise in Japan's birth rate would be insufficient, however, to prevent the shrinking of the population or, especially, of the working-age population. That reality becomes immediately apparent from an objective analysis of the nation's demographic profile. As for hosting foreign workers, inflows of labor on any realistically conceivable scale would be insufficient to prevent economic shrinkage.

This work suggests ways for Japanese to maintain a comfortable standard of living amid the inevitable demographic and economic trends. All of the economic issues posed by population shrinkage and aging are surmountable. In fact, demographic trends and the socioeconomic changes that they occasion can be opportunities to redress Japan's biggest economic flaw: the failure of economic growth to produce commensurate improvements in the quality of life. Demographic trends will provide a platform for addressing that issue.

A new mind-set, to be sure, will be necessary. Individuals, industry, and government will need to abandon their traditional fixation with growth. The scenario outlined at the opening of this text is the result of the new mind-set. That scenario is my notion of an abundant society.

The Koizumi government has presented its agenda for administrative and economic reform as a precondition for lasting economic growth. But as we have seen, Japan's economy will begin to contract sooner or later, no matter what policies the nation adopts. Reworking Japan's administrative and economic machinery on the false premise of ensuring economic expansion endangers the nation's long-term economic health. A more-responsible approach would start with considering measures for ensuring socioeconomic vitality amid economic contraction. Policy makers would then determine what kind of infrastructure those measures will require, and they would take appropriate action.

Population shrinkage and its economic implications are a research focus of long standing for me, and this work follows my *Jinko Gensho Shakai no Sekkei* (*A Design for a Shrinking-Population Society*) published by Chuokoron-Shinsha, Inc., in 2002. That work presented the broad outlines of Japan's socioeconomic future. This work proposes more-concrete responses for individuals, for companies, for regions, and for the national government. I offer this new work in the hope of clearing away the fog of misunderstanding that envelops demographic issues and nudging the national discourse toward real and substantive issues. Demographic change presents huge opportunities for Japan and for Japanese. Fulfilling those opportunities needs to begin with understanding and addressing the real issues at hand.

Tokyo
May 2004

Author's Introduction to the English (2006) Edition

In 2005, Japan became the world's pioneer in shrinking-population socioeconomics. It became the first large industrialized nation to experience a population decline as a result of natural causes. Continuing population growth has been an automatic assumption in economics for as long as anyone can remember, and the implications of population shrinkage are huge and far-reaching. Japan's economic and social systems—holdovers from an era of continuing population expansion—will become dysfunctional in the era of population shrinkage. The new demographic realities will force a thorough revamping of those systems.

Japanese will need to do without familiar tools as they tackle the task of reengineering their socioeconomic infrastructure. The social sciences offer little in the way of practical mechanisms for coping with population shrinkage. Simply reversing the formulas used for dealing with expanding economies does not necessarily make them applicable to a shrinking economy.

New perspectives will be essential as Japanese contend with unprecedented demographic change. All too many people in positions of influence refuse to see the inevitability of shrinkage in the workforce and in the population overall. Instead of acknowledging that inevitability and addressing it responsibly, they seek to avoid the unavoidable. They call for encouraging childbearing, for example, and for recruiting foreign labor, neither of which is likely to reverse population shrinkage or prevent economic contraction. Their stance is understandable, considering that they owe their positions of influence to the old order. Their Luddite response is a natural reaction to trends that will destroy that order.

Japanese will gradually recognize the inescapability of population shrinkage and of its twin, economic contraction. But they need to get started soon on serious initiatives for overhauling their nation's social and economic systems. They need to reshape those systems to maintain socioeconomic vitality and abundance amid the new demographic and economic realities. That will include rethinking the meaning of vitality and abundance in light of changing values.

The shift from population growth to population shrinkage is a transition of epochal proportions. Japan is entirely capable of coping with that transition, however, as long as it adopts sound policies.

I published this work in 2004 to air some policy proposals for Japan. Population shrinkage will also occur in Europe, in the Americas, and in Asian nations besides Japan in the years and decades ahead. Coping with the profound implications of demographic change will require a massive, long-term reworking of socioeconomic infrastructure. I hope that this work will be of value beyond Japan in shedding light on the issues at hand and in highlighting realistic policy options.

Tokyo
February 2006

CHAPTER I

All at Once:
The Coming Post-Max World

JAPAN'S JOLTING TRANSITION TO
A SHRINKING, AGING SOCIETY

SWIFT DEMOGRAPHIC CHANGE AS THE LEGACY OF RAPID ECONOMIC GROWTH

Japanese society is aging at a pace unprecedented in any large nation. Demographers characterize societies where people older than 65 constitute more than 7% of the population as aging societies, and they refer to societies where the over-65 percentage is greater than 14% as aged societies. By those criteria, Japanese society went from aging to aged in the stunningly brief span of only 24 years. The over-65 component of Japan's population reached 7% in 1970 and 14% in 1994.

In contrast, the same transition took 40 years in Germany and 47 years in the United Kingdom. France's transition from aging to aged took even longer. The over-65 percentage of the French population reached 7% way back in 1864, but it didn't reach 14% until 115 years later, in 1979. In the United States, people older than 65 first accounted for more than 7% of the population in 1942. As of 2004, more than 60 years later, the over-65 percentage of U.S. society was only 12.5%.

The aging of society is a phenomenon common to all industrialized nations, but it is proceeding a lot faster in Japan than anywhere else. And the reason for that disparity is the dramatic lengthening of life expectancy that occurred in postwar Japan. In 1947, the average life expectancy in Japan was 50.1 years for males and 54.0 for females. In 1970, the figures were 69.3 years for males and 74.7 for females. Japanese life expectancy

1

thus surged some 20 years in a mere 23-year interval. During approximately the same interval, the average life expectancy for males and females combined increased only 3.5 years in Germany, to 71.0 in 1970, from 67.5 in 1950, and only 5.9 years in France, to 72.4, from 66.5. Life expectancy increased only 2.8 years in the United States and only 2.3 years in the United Kingdom in that same time span.

Just as striking as the speed of Japan's gains in life expectancy has been the impressive length that Japanese life spans have attained. Average life spans for Japanese in the early postwar years were way below the "old-age" benchmark of 65. The sharp increase in life expectancy propelled Japanese life spans to well over that benchmark in the blink of an eye.

Driving Japan's swift growth in life expectancy has been a huge increase in the number of people older than 65. That number nearly doubled, to 7.3 million in 1970, from 3.7 million in 1947. In 1994, the number of over-65 Japanese was 17.6 million, up 4.7-fold over the 1947 figure. Meanwhile, Japan's total population had grown only 30% over the 1947 total by 1970 and just 60% by 1994.

Underlying the surge in Japanese life spans was Japan's rapid economic growth. Economic expansion raises personal incomes, helping people enjoy healthier diets and better living conditions in general. Economic growth supports improvements in medical care, too, which also contribute to longer lives. Before World War II, Japan ranked economically somewhere between the industrialized and developing worlds. The nation's postwar "economic miracle" transformed it seemingly overnight into an advanced economy. Conditions that figure in average life span underwent a profound transformation for the better. The magnitude of that transformation has no parallel in the experience of the United States, the United Kingdom, Germany, or France. All of those nations were already industrialized economies before World War II, and all of them had attained an average life expectancy in excess of 65 years.

JAPAN'S UNIQUE DEMOGRAPHICS

By 1998, Japan had become the oldest society on earth, and it is poised to continue aging faster than any other nation (figure 1). That outlook is on the basis of the mortality rate and birthrate in each age stratum. Any

Figure 1

The Over-65 Percentage of the Population in Principal Industrialized Nations–
Past, Present, and Future

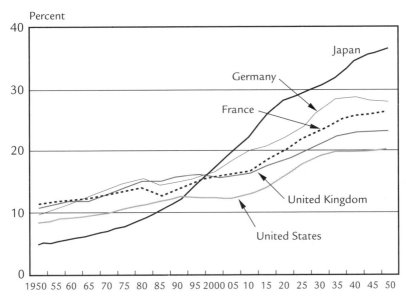

Source: United Nations, *World Population Prospects 2002 Revised*

change in the projected trends for those rates will affect the outlook for the overall size of the population and for the over-65 percentage of the total. We need to be careful, of course, to use consistent statistical methodologies in comparing population forecasts for different nations. The United Nations, the source of the data in figure 1, tends to understate mortality rates in its early data on age strata. Japan's National Institute of Population and Social Security Research, meanwhile, tends to overstate birthrates.

Figure 1 indicates a pronounced and continuing increase in the percentage of Japanese older than 65. The projected aging of Japanese society is substantially faster than in other industrialized nations up to around 2015 and after 2030. That is due to Japan's unique demographics rather than to the longevity gains that formerly drove the nation's aging. Japan's average life expectancy reached 78.1 years for males and 84.9 for females in 2001. At those already-high levels, Japanese longevity will naturally grow more slowly than in the past, and we will see a convergence among industrialized nations in the pace of gains in life expectancy.

We can see what is unique about Japan's demographics in figure 2. The graph compares the structure of populations in representative industrialized nations by age group. For each nation, it shows the population weighting of each age stratum as a percentage deviation from the average weighting for all age strata. Two precipitous peaks are prominent in Japan's demographic profile. They are corollaries of Japan's postwar baby boom and its follow-up boom. The demographic profile for each nation includes a peak that corresponds to a postwar baby boom, but we see little in the way of counterparts to Japan's second baby boom. In addition, the peaks for the United States, the United Kingdom, and France are lower and less steep than Japan's; only Germany presents a comparably precipitous peak.

The prominent trough between Japan's two baby boom peaks is a unique and defining feature of Japanese demographics. It is the chief reason that society will continue aging substantially faster in Japan than in other industrialized nations. Each of the demographic profiles in figure 2 moves to the right with the passage of time. The aging of society will accelerate in each nation as the baby boomers reach 65. But over-65 baby boomers will account for a larger percentage of the population in Japan than elsewhere. That's because the trough in Japan's demographic profile amplifies the relative weighting of the peaks.

Another defining characteristic of Japanese demographics is the fluctuating pace at which the aging of society will progress. Japan's population will age rapidly until around 2015. That is when the demographic peak on the right in figure 2 will reach the age of 65. Japan's aging will then slow for awhile, but it will accelerate again as the left peak in figure 2 approaches the age of 65 in the 2030s. As before, the sharp demographic drop-off to the left of the peak will amplify the over-65 weighting in the population.

ECHOES OF ZEALOUS BIRTH CONTROL

Japan's precipitous demographic peaks reflect the brevity of the nation's baby boom. In most other industrialized nations, the baby boom continued for well over 10 years. Japan's baby boom ended in barely 4 years, terminated by an aggressive program of birth control. The centerpiece of that program was the Eugenic Protection Act (Yuseihogoho) of 1948. As

Figure 2

Population Composition by Age in Principal Industrialized Nations in 2000

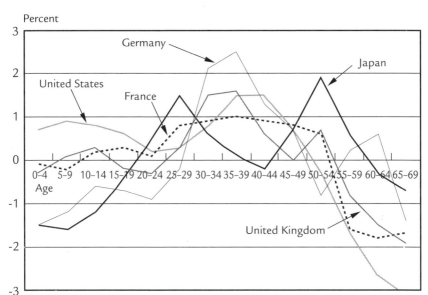

Source: United Nations, *World Population Prospects 2002 Revised*

revised in 1949, that law essentially sanctioned abortion on demand. That resulted in a sudden decline of about 40% in Japan's birthrate and put an early end to the nation's baby boom.

The Eugenic Protection Act remains a controversial chapter in Japanese history, partly because of its eugenically discriminatory measures, which since have been eliminated. We need to note, however, that postwar Japan was contending with the privations that followed crushing defeat in World War II and that zealous birth control was part of a national struggle for survival. We must also note cultural differences in the demographic divergence between Japan and nations where Christian values impeded the practice of abortion. Whatever our views on Japan's postwar population policy, the nation must live with the continuing ramifications of that policy.

Germany also presents a steep demographic peak in figure 2. That peak, however, is the result of immigration policy rather than birth control. After the east-west partition of Germany, a labor shortage occurred in the west and prompted officials to welcome a huge influx of foreign workers. The West German government subsequently restricted immigration in response to the mounting social cost of a burgeoning foreign population.

Japan's initial population peak preceded Germany's peak by about 15 years. Germany will thus experience a surge in the over-65 percentage of its population about 15 years after Japan does. In the mid-2030s, people older than 65 will account for a similar percentage of the population in Germany as in Japan. But the aging of society will then resume proceeding faster in Japan than in Germany. That is because of Japan's distinctive, second demographic peak.

We have seen that Japan shifted from an aging society (7% of the population older than 65) to an aged society (14% over 65) in the unparalleled brief span of just 24 years. But the further aging of Japanese society will proceed just as fast. The over-65 percentage of Japanese will reach 28%—double the "aged" demographic threshold—shortly before 2020. Japan's over-65 surge to 28% of the population, from 14%, will occur in approximately the same quarter-century span as the increase to 14%, from 7%.

AGING AS A FACTOR IN POPULATION DECLINE

An absolute decline in population will accompany the aging of Japanese society. Quite simply, the number of people dying will outnumber the number of people being born. Observers commonly attribute this impending differential to the Japanese trend toward smaller families. But that trend is only part of the answer. Equally important is the impending surge in Japan's mortality rate. Principally because of that surge, the population decline in Japan will be sharp.

The mortality rate in Japan displayed a pronounced upturn in the late 1990s. Mortality had declined amid rapid gains in life expectancy, and the annual number of Japanese deaths remained flat even as the over-65 component of the population expanded rapidly. Even Japanese remain mortal, however, and the burgeoning number of elderly Japanese ultimately occasioned an upturn in the mortality rate.

Demographics dictate that Japan's mortality rate will continue to rise. It will rise rapidly until the first-generation baby boomers reach the end of their average life expectancy around 2030. Note that in figure 3 the

Figure 3
Births, Deaths, and the Over-65 Population in Japan

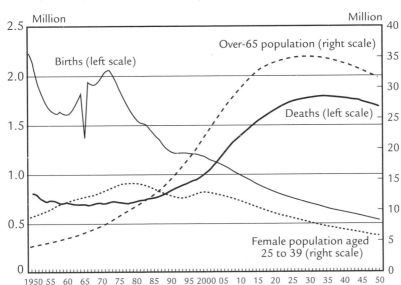

Sources: National census data published by the Statistics Bureau of Japan's Ministry of
    Internal Affairs and Communications for years to 2000 and projections by
    Fujimasa Iwao for subsequent years

growth trend in mortality is conspicuously steeper than the downward
trend in births. Annual births, though lower than during the baby booms,
are declining at only a moderate pace. Clearly, a sharp rise in mortality will
be the main reason for the alarming velocity of Japan's impending population shrinkage.

Some Japanese have called for measures to encourage women to have
more children. But any such measures would be wholly insufficient to
match the rise in mortality. For one thing, the number of Japanese women
of childbearing age is entering a period of sustained decline. For another,
the decline in the birthrate (average births per woman) is a long-standing trend of powerful, deep-rooted momentum. That decline has continued since the 1920s, reflecting social progress, changing attitudes among
women, advances in health care, and other factors. A sudden reversal in
the overall trend is inconceivable.

That a population begins to shrink when the birthrate declines below
2.1 has become a widely known axiom of demographics. However, that

rule of thumb pertains most usefully to extremely long-term population trends. The dominant factor by far in Japan's population decline over the next 50 years or so will be the aging of society.

A 40 MILLION DECLINE IN A HALF-CENTURY

Let us examine Japan's impending population decline through statistics prepared by Professor Fujimasa Iwao, a colleague of the author at Japan's National Graduate Institute for Policy Studies. As noted elsewhere in this book, U.N. statistics tend to understate mortality rates. That presents no problem in examining trends among nations from a relative perspective, since the U.N. methodology is consistent. Professor Fujimasa's statistics support greater accuracy, however, in examining absolute trends in Japan. In addition, economic and fiscal projections require more-detailed population statistics than the United Nations has prepared or has published. For the same reason, Professor Fujimasa's statistics are preferable to the statistics published by Japan's National Institute of Population and Social Security Research.

Figure 4 expresses Japanese demographic trends as calculated by Professor Fujimasa. The population in 2030, at 108 million, is 14.0%—nearly 18 million people—lower than in 2000. In 2050, it has declined 32.4%—nearly 41 million people—to 85 million. Japan experienced population growth unprecedented for a developed nation in the half-century to 2000. From about 83 million in 1950, the population grew more than 50%. It will now shrink approximately the same numerical amount over the next half-century. And that stunning decline is unavoidable because it will result mainly from the demographic profile of people already alive. The aging of society will occasion a sharp increase in mortality. The coming stark decline in population is thus a pressing issue for Japanese in drafting economic policy and in designing social programs.

DEMOGRAPHIC ARTIFICE IN JAPAN AND GERMANY

All of the large industrialized nations are experiencing gains in life expectancy and declines in family size. Trends in overall population, however, are less consistent, at least for the coming generation—about 30 years. Japan and Germany are the only large industrialized nations that will have small-

Figure 4
Over-65 Japanese

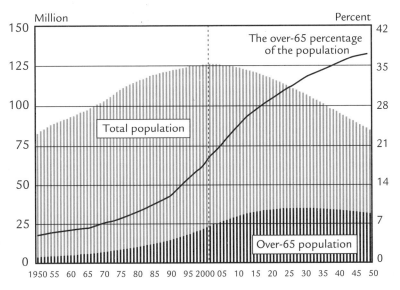

Sources: National census data published by the Statistics Bureau of Japan's Ministry of
    Internal Affairs and Communications for years to 2000 and projections by
    Fujimasa Iwao for subsequent years

er populations in 2030 than in 2000. Society is aging faster in Japan and
Germany than in other industrialized nations (figure 1), and those two
nations will have correspondingly greater increases in mortality.

As we have seen, the aging of society in Japan and in Germany is the
echo of earlier policy decisions: the decision in Japan to promote birth
control through the extensive practice of abortion; the decision in Germany
to welcome large numbers of foreign workers and the subsequent German
decision to restrict inward immigration. Japan and Germany are the only
industrialized nations that have systematically adjusted their population
size through policy artifice. But any artificial interference with demographic trends produces repercussions, and that is exactly what is hap-
pening in Japan and Germany. And Japan's population decline will be
even faster than Germany's because its population is aging faster.

No developed nation has ever experienced a large, long-term decline
in population. Japan is thus destined to be a demographic pioneer in the
uncharted waters of negative population growth.

Japan as the Slowest-Growth Economy

A Population Trough as a Factor in High Economic Growth

Japan's distinctive, twin-peaked demographic profile figured prominently in the nation's postwar economic miracle. That profile helped overcome a barrier to economic growth that occurs commonly in developing and rebuilding economies. Rising incomes in emerging economies typically occasion higher birthrates, rapid population growth, and attendant surges in consumption demand. Domestic savings are insufficient to finance enough capital spending to serve rising demand, imports increase, and current account balances deteriorate.

Unable to countenance current account deficits indefinitely, governments resort to measures for curtailing demand, and that undercuts the incipient development of domestic industry. This pattern all too often prevents nations from achieving sustainable development momentum.

Postwar Japan was essentially an emerging economy, since it had lost a lot of its productive capacity in the war. And concerns about the international balance of payments retarded economic growth somewhat in Japan until the late 1960s. Those concerns, however, were not so serious as to prevent the sound development of domestic industry. That is largely because Japan had attained a high level of economic development before the war and because the nation enjoyed a high rate of savings. Japan was therefore able to avoid the problem of insufficient domestic funding for capital spending that plagues developing nations.

If Japan had spent all of its annual domestic income on consumption, funding would have been unavailable for capital spending, and the nation's productive capacity would not have resumed growing. Japanese industry was able to invest as much—and only as much—in expanding production capacity as Japanese put aside in savings. Borrowing from abroad was not a long-term option, since net capital inflows would require corresponding and unsustainable current account deficits.

The standard measure of economic growth is gross domestic product (GDP), and a high savings rate is essential to GDP growth. Postwar Japan was able to maintain a high savings rate because its population

Figure 5
The Working-Age Percentage of the Population in
Principal Industrialized Nations

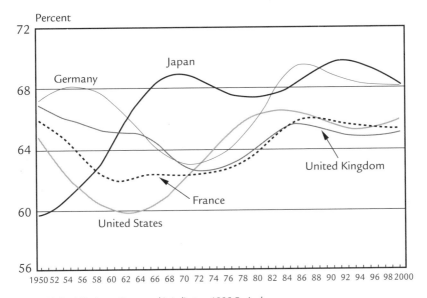

Source: United Nations, *Demographic Indicators 1998 Revised*

growth, though high for an industrialized nation, was low by develop-ing world standards. Japan's birthrate during its initial baby boom was 3.4, which is as high as the birthrates typical of developing nations. But that baby boom ended, as we have seen, in only about 4 years. If it had last-ed more than 10 years, Japan would have had a population explosion like developing nations do. The high savings rate and the high-paced eco-nomic growth that it supported would have been impossible.

Figure 5 shows the working-age (15 to 64) population as a percent-age of the total population in five industrialized nations. That percent-age declined through the postwar years in the United States and in the European nations. Only in Japan did it grow steadily.

National savings mirror the working-age percentage of the popula-tion, just as family savings reflect the number of household wage earn-ers. Japan's savings rate thus rose in the postwar era and surpassed the U.S. and European rates in the early 1960s. The savings rate in Japan remained high for several more years, though it began to decline after the working-age percentage of the population stopped growing in the early 1970s.

We now see how the twin peaks and the intervening trough in Japan's demographic profile (figure 1) made possible the nation's economic miracle. The trough resulted from the abrupt and early end of the initial baby boom. It meant that the nonproductive, under-age population was small in comparison with the working-age population in the postwar years. That allowed the savings rate to rise rapidly and enabled Japan to achieve robust industrial and economic development without incurring unsustainable deficits in the international balance of payments.

Of course, the rise in the working-age percentage of the Japanese population also reflected growth in the absolute number of working-age citizens. That growth resulted from a national campaign of encouraging reproduction in the second decade of the century. Japan's earlier encouragement and later discouragement of reproduction combined to create an optimal demographic profile for rebuilding from the ashes of defeat. That profile positioned Japan to make the most of the technology, the priority production systems, and the management methods that industry and government would cooperate in deploying.

JAPAN'S DEMOGRAPHIC TROUGH AS A FUTURE WEIGHT ON ECONOMIC GROWTH

What goes around comes around, however, and the same demographic profile that supported rapid economic growth will now begin to weigh heavily on Japan's economy. In fact, it will leave Japan with the lowest rate of economic growth among the large industrialized nations. GDP requires labor to grow. A nation can have abundant savings, and it can pour those savings into expanded production capacity. But that will not add anything to GDP in the absence of labor for putting the capacity to work.

The size of a nation's GDP ultimately depends heavily on the size of the nation's workforce. Labor productivity varies among nations, of course, and nations can increase their economic output by deploying technology and by raising economic efficiency in other ways. But differentials in labor productivity among the industrialized nations are small.

Labor productivity is essentially a function of (1) the amount of labor necessary to operate each machine and (2) the hourly output of each

Figure 6
Annual Percentage Change in the Working-Age Percentage of the
Population in Principal Industrialized Nations

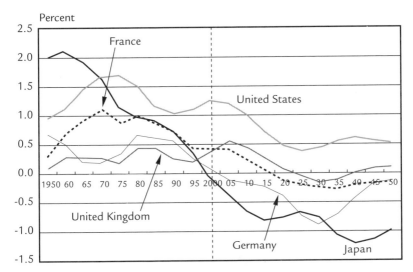

Source: United Nations, *World Population Prospects 2002 Revised*

machine. We find little difference among the industrialized nations in regard to these two criteria. Economic globalization means that technological advances soon disseminate throughout the world.

So we can regard differences in GDP among the industrialized nations as mirror images of differences in working-age population. And we can regard differentials in economic growth rates as direct reflections of differentials in working-age population growth.

Figure 6 presents U.N. statistical data for the growth rates of the working-age populations in our sample of industrialized nations. U.N. statistics are adequate for this purpose because the issue at hand is relative and the tendency of U.N. data to understate mortality rates in its early data on age strata is thus irrelevant. We need to bear in mind that "working-age population" is not identical to the number of people actually working. But history indicates that the working-age population and the workforce in each nation follow basically the same trends over the long term. So we can regard the former as a reliable determinant of economic growth.

Japan's working-age population has been declining since 1995, and it will continue to decline for the foreseeable future. Germany will be the next of the five industrialized nations to experience a decline in working-age population, but the rate of decline in Germany will be small until around 2020. Germany's working-age population will not begin to decline sharply until after 2020, and the rate of decline there will slow greatly in the 2030s. France's and the United Kingdom's working-age populations will cross over into negative growth around 2020, but the rate of decline in each nation will be extremely small. The United States has an extremely young demographic profile, and its working-age population will continue to grow for decades to come.

Trends in working-age population suggest strongly that Japan will have the slowest economic growth among the large industrialized nations. They suggest equally strongly that the differentials in economic growth rates will be large. For instance, nearly two percentage points separate the trend lines for working-age population in Japan and the United States over the next 10-some years.

A common rebuttal to this scenario cites the relatively low percentage of Japanese women employed or seeking employment outside the home. This counterargument asserts that an increasing percentage of Japanese women will opt to join the workforce and that Japan's actual working population will not decline as much as figure 6 indicates. The International Labor Organization reports that the percentage of women older than 20 employed or seeking employment outside the home in 1998 was 63.9% in Japan, compared with 72.5% in the United States (*Year Book of Labor Statistics 1998*). That disparity might seem to support the rebuttal. However, the differential between the average annual growth rates for Japan's actual working population and its working-age population since 1975—a period during which the percentage of working women has increased markedly—has been less than 0.4%. Even if we raise the trend line for Japan in figure 6 by that amount, the line remains well below the U.S. trend line and below the lines for the United Kingdom and France.

We also need to recognize that the percentage of working women will rise in other nations too, though not necessarily by the same amount. The percentage of women employed outside the home is higher in Japan than in Germany or France and about the same level as in the United Kingdom.

Meanwhile, the average age of the working-age population is rising a great deal faster in Japan than in other nations. That is a result of the faster pace of the aging of society overall in Japan, and it could actually reduce the working percentage of Japanese women.

We thus have every reason to assume that the workforce is about to shrink more rapidly in Japan than in any other large industrialized nation. The gaping trough between Japan's two population peaks is progressing inexorably across the nation's demographic profile. It is already diminishing the working-age population, and it will leave Japan with the lowest economic growth rate among the large industrialized nations.

Maxed Out

All too fast

The wrenching demographic change in store for Japan will do worse than slow the pace of economic growth; it will shrink the nation's economy. Negative economic growth will become the norm in the nation that until recently set the pace for the industrialized world. That is because of the all-too-rapid pace of Japan's aging and of its population decline. The aging of society at a more moderate pace, as in France, would not push the economy into negative growth. Even Germany, whose demographic profile is more similar to Japan's, appears likely to enjoy positive economic growth for another 20 years or so.

Technological progress raises labor productivity. Japan's continuing advances in technology would offset the economic effects of a moderate decline in the workforce and support continuing GDP growth. The problem is that Japan's working-age population will shrink far too fast for the decline to be offset through technological advances and resultant gains in labor productivity.

The all-too-rapid pace of Japan's aging is also the villain in the nation's pension system drama. Everything would be a lot more manageable if the aging of Japanese society was proceeding a little more slowly. As things stand, the number of people who pay into the system will decline sharply even as the number of people who receive benefits increases rapidly. Something has got to give soon and in a big way. Japan will need to increase premiums, reduce benefits, or devise some combination of the two. The outlook for pension systems is also a concern in European nations, but the problem there is nowhere near as severe as in Japan. That is because the pace of change in the populations of payers and beneficiaries is far more moderate.

Being told that pension benefits might decline 10% or 20% during your lifetime is one thing. Hearing that they will decline 50% or more is something else again. People typically expect to receive pension benefits for around 25 years at most. "During your lifetime" is an awfully brief span for such a profound shift in ground rules. Pensioners and soon-to-be pensioners are in the front lines of Japan's all-too-sudden shift in demographics.

What is especially important for Japanese today is to come to terms with the inevitability of that shift. Even a miraculous upturn in the birthrate would not turn the tide. A surge of infants would not begin to augment the workforce for nearly a quarter-century. And in the meantime, those infants would aggravate Japan's economic woes. The burgeoning ranks of dependents would depress Japan's savings rate further and worsen the economic downturn. They would also undermine the financial capacity of the contributors to Japan's pension system.

Too many commentators in Japan continue to cite the declining birthrate as a cause of the nation's population-related problems. That analysis is flawed because it diverts attention from the fundamental issue— an inevitable and rapid decline in population caused by a rising mortality rate among people already alive—and because it implies wrongly that future trends in the birthrate and other factors could somehow reverse the population decline and its economic and social ramifications. It also fails to acknowledge Japan's economic debt to the postwar program of drastic birth control.

FOREIGN WORKERS AS A NONSOLUTION

Importing foreign workers strikes a lot of observers as a natural solution to Japan's coming labor shortage. Until the 1980s, the debate about the desirability of foreign labor centered on professionals and individuals who possessed special skills. The focus of debate has shifted, however, to manual laborers and other low-wage workers. Hunting for low-wage labor seems an odd pursuit for a nation more accustomed to seeking corporate growth and economic progress through technological innovation. But the author is unqualified to expound on labor issues and will concentrate instead on the demographic implications of foreign labor.

Low-wage manual laborers from abroad would presumably be mainly in the 20s and 30s age brackets. Those brackets correspond in Japan to the secondary baby boom, the left peak in figure 2. So manual laborers in their 20s and 30s who came and stayed would simply aggravate the demographic problems presented by that peak. Japan might possibly benefit from an influx of labor to fill the trough between its two demographic peaks. That could help smooth the pace of the aging of Japanese society. Immigrants for fulfilling that need, however, would be in their late 40s. That might be a viable age bracket for professionals and highly skilled workers from overseas, but a large influx of manual laborers in that age bracket is inconceivable.

The left peak in figure 2 is thus the crux of the problem from a demographic perspective. Admitting large numbers of foreign workers on a continuing, long-term basis would create a gentler slope on the left side of the peak and could soften the economic and social disruption caused by the peak. But the experience of Germany suggests that an influx of foreign workers would become untenable at some point and that Japan would then shut the door. That would create an even more precipitous slope down the left side of the peak.

We have seen that the trough between the two peaks in figure 2 will be responsible for the rapid shrinkage and aging of Japan's population and for the related problems of negative economic growth and a funding shortfall in the pension system. An ill-considered immigration policy could create another trough to the left of the second peak and cause even-bigger problems 20 years down the line.

In conclusion, foreign workers are a stopgap solution that would simply postpone Japan's demographic day of reckoning. They might allow Japan to forestall the shift to negative economic growth. They might even alleviate the funding shortfall in the nation's pension system. But like government bonds issued to fund fiscal deficits, they would simply shift the problem to future generations. To whatever extent they alleviated problems for Japan today, they would magnify the problems of economic decline and pension underfunding that will confront posterity.

A possible counterargument is that Japan should soften the disruptive effects of sudden demographic change by spreading them across generations. However, the people who deserve the right to refute that argument are the Japanese children of today and their yet-unborn children of tomorrow. They are the ones who would contend with the new demographic trough created by a German-like reversal of immigration policy. The debate needs to address the interests of those people who as of yet lack a political voice of their own.

MASSIVE STRUCTURAL CHANGE

Japan is headed for several decades of population decline. That decline will continue long after the end of the sharp decline associated with the passing of the baby boom generation. In no industrialized nation do we find a birthrate higher than the 2.1 needed to maintain population size, and we have no reason to believe that Japan's birthrate will return to even that level.

Statistics for different nations reveal a strong correlation between the aging of society and a declining birthrate. The reasons for that correlation are unclear. It could be part of some biological mechanism. Perhaps humans are programmed to have fewer babies to offset the population growth that results from longevity gains. That mechanism could be something unique to human groups that have evolved advanced societies and developed sophisticated medical technology.

This book will examine the prospects for Japanese society and the Japanese economy after they have lost the energizing dynamism of continuing population growth. The nation has operated socially and economically on the assumption of continuing population growth. Now, Japan has reached its population maximum (figure 4), and the post-max era will be a time of unprecedented structural change.

That change will be jarringly sudden. The all-too-rapid shrinking and aging of Japan's population will thrust the nation brusquely into that post-max era. Japanese will need to accommodate the new realities in personal planning, in management strategy, and in public policy.

As stunningly swift as the change will seem initially, it will accelerate. The rate of population decline will increase annually. Stopgap solutions will soon prove wholly inadequate. Only systematic social and economic restructuring based on a long-term perspective can position Japan to cope with the post-max era.

The necessary restructuring will inevitably encounter resistance from vested interests that would cling to the old social and economic structures. Those interests will push frantically for measures that offer even the slightest hope of forestalling the shrinking and aging of Japan's population. They will call for efforts to raise the birthrate and for initiatives to encourage inflows of foreign labor.

No artifice, however, can prevent the impending decrease in the size of the Japanese population. And time is short. Japan can ill afford any further delay in preparing for the inevitable. In the next year or two, Japan will enter a phase of irreversible population decline. The time to act is now.

CHAPTER II

Expansion Becomes Shrinkage: Wrenching Change in the Business Environment

A ONE-THIRD REDUCTION IN AVAILABLE LABOR

INEVITABLE CHANGE IN THE WORKING PERCENTAGE OF THE POPULATION

We saw in chapter 1 that Japan's working-age population is destined to decline. We saw that the decline in Japan's working-age population will produce the lowest economic growth rate among the industrialized nations and that the Japanese economy will shrink inexorably over the long term. In chapter 2, we will examine just how much Japan's economy can be expected to shrink. We need to begin by projecting trends in the amount of labor that will be available.

Our first task is to decide how much the economically active percentage of the population is likely to rise. Here, economically active refers to people who have the desire to work. The desire to work outside the home has become increasingly common among Japanese women in recent years, and the economically active percentage of the female population has risen correspondingly. Meanwhile, Japan's average life span has lengthened greatly, and that encourages the view that a growing number of Japanese will continue working into old age.

The Statistics Bureau in Japan's Ministry of Internal Affairs and Communications employs a narrow definition of desire to work in calculating the economically active population. It restricts the definition to people who are actually working or who are actively seeking work. By this definition, economically active does not include, for example, a mother who wants a job but who lacks access to a day care center for her young child and has therefore not sought employment.

Nor does the definition encompass elderly people who possess the desire to work but who have not sought work. Numerous Japanese fit this description because prospective employers are unreceptive to older job applicants and because Japan lacks a social framework for promoting the extensive employment of elderly people. Economic forecasts require an accurate grasp of the amount of labor that will actually be available, and the Statistics Bureau's definition is a reasonable one from that perspective.

We thus need to recognize that trends in the economically active population are highly subject to developments in social infrastructure, as well as to individual disposition. We need to recognize, too, that the will to work is a highly personal consideration, and that it reflects differences in attitudes and in lifestyles. All of this is to say that we encounter numerous uncertainties in preparing forecasts of the economically active population. Forecasters commonly resort to a methodology in which they assume that present trends will continue.

Underlying this methodology is the recognition that changes in people's attitudes and in social frameworks and systems tend to occur not in sudden shifts but in continuing, incremental trends. Of course, forecasters also have the option of employing economic models based on the functional analysis of labor supply. But models are of questionable value in long-term forecasting, where we need to account for change in people's attitudes and in the social fabric. They are the stuff of economic theory, and economics lacks adequate measures for personal and social phenomena.

PAST DEVELOPMENTS IN THE ECONOMICALLY ACTIVE PERCENTAGE OF THE POPULATION

Forecasting based on trends depends, by definition, on being able to identify patterns in past developments—patterns clear enough for any observer to discern. But we need to be careful to identify trends separately by gender and by age. For instance, the percentage of women who desire employment declines through the age spectrum from late 20s to early 40s, the years of childbearing and child rearing. And few people of either

Figure 7

The Economically Active Percentage of Working-Age Men and Women
and Elderly in Japan

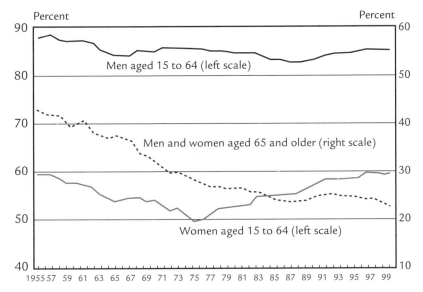

Source: Labor survey data published by the Statistics Bureau of Japan's Ministry of
Internal Affairs and Communications

gender retain a strong urge to work after they reach the age of 75.

Figure 7 presents past trends in the economically active percentage
of the Japanese population. The percentage is relatively steady among
males aged 15 to 64, but we see clear patterns of change in the percentages among females in that age range and among people of both genders
aged 65 and older. The author has used broad age spectrums in this figure for simplicity of presentation. Identical patterns are evident, though,
in the original data, which covers different age strata in 10-year age increments, and by gender. So the trends visible here furnish a reliable basis
for forecasting.

The trends in the economically active percentage of Japan's population
change noticeably in the mid-1970s for women and for elderly people of
both genders. For women aged 15 to 64, the prolonged downward trend
gives way to an upturn. And for over-65 people of both genders, the pace
of decline slows visibly. These changes are partly attributable to the rapid
decline in agriculture that occurred in the preceding years. Note, however,

that the economically active percentage of the over-65 population continues to decline, albeit at a slower pace than before. That is because the number of upper-aged elderly—people older than 75—grew as a result of the increase in average life span. In other words, an increase occurred in the number of people physically unsuited to work on account of advanced age.

A SHARPER DECLINE IN THE ECONOMICALLY ACTIVE POPULATION THAN IN THE OVERALL POPULATION

The author has calculated future trends in the economically active percentage of the population by gender and by 10-year age stratum. He has projected the future trends mathematically on the basis of trends since 1975. Figure 8 presents the author's projections for the economically active population as an absolute number and as a percentage of the overall population to 2030. The economically active population is poised to decline to 54.7 million people in 2030, from 67.7 million in 2000—a decline of 13 million people, or 19.2%.

We hear calls for offsetting the effect of population decline on Japan's workforce by promoting employment opportunities for women and for elderly people of both genders. But no reasonably imaginable increase in the employment of women and of the elderly can prevent the economically active population from declining faster than the overall population. In figure 8, the author has assumed continuing upward trends in the economically active percentage of women aged 15 to 64 and of lower-aged elderly of both genders—ages 65 to 74. Yet the projected decline in the economically active population from 2000 to 2030 is still sharper than the projected 14.0% decline in the overall population. The economically active percentage of Japanese older than 15 will decline precipitously and will reach its lowest level ever.

Most actual labor, by far, belongs to the 15-to-64 range commonly identified as working age. And the rapid aging of Japanese society will cause the population in that age range to decline faster than the overall population. That differential is also readily apparent in figure 8. The decline in working-age population between 2000 and 2030, at 27.8%, is nearly double the 14.0% decline in overall population.

The growing proportion of nonworking people in the population

Figure 8

Japan's Working-Age Population and Economically Active Population

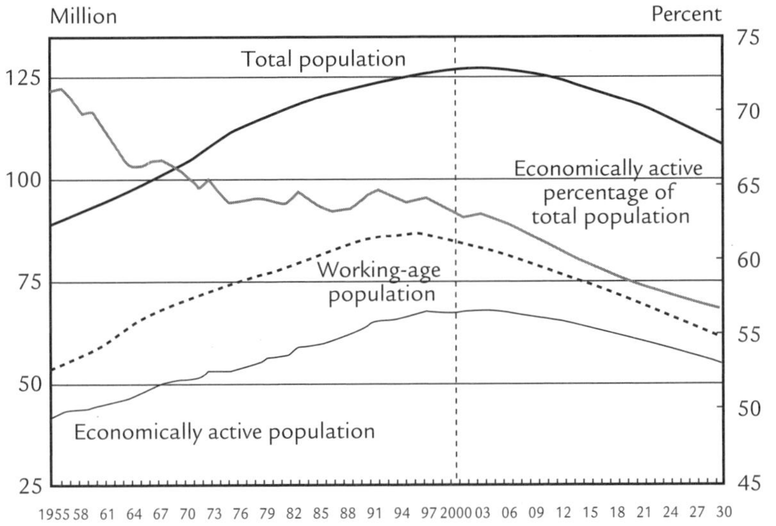

Sources: National census data and labor survey data published by the Statistics Bureau of
     Japan's Ministry of Internal Affairs and Communications for the years to 2000
     and, for subsequent years, projections by Fujimasa Iwao for total population and
     working-age population and projections by the author for the economically active
     percentage of the total population

presents issues for Japan's pension program and for other social programs, as noted in chapter 1. But we must be wary of proposals for
addressing those issues by putting more women and old people to work.
The issues are structural and will arise despite a growing propensity to
work among women and among lower-aged elderly of both genders.
Japan has good reasons—social and humanitarian—to provide employment opportunities for the growing range of citizens eager to work. But
the notion of resolving the nation's fiscal problems by mobilizing the populace is ludicrous—an anachronous echo of the wartime National
Mobilization Law.

SHORTER WORKING HOURS

Calculating the labor input for economic forecasts requires assumptions
about working hours per person, as well as about the size of the workforce.
Any change in average hours worked has the same economic effect as an

identical percentage change in the workforce. And average monthly working hours per person in Japan have been declining for several years, as shown in figure 9.

Japan has reduced the average annual working hours per person by establishing a five-day workweek, by increasing the number of national holidays, and through other measures. The Japanese initiatives have been part of a global trend, spearheaded by the International Labor Organization, toward shorter working hours. Despite Japan's initiatives, the nation still has a longer average workweek than other large industrialized nations. The average workweek in Japan in the 1990s was 43.7 hours. That was substantially longer than Germany's 38.3 hours and France's 38.7 hours. It was even longer than the United States' 41.4 hours.

The International Labor Organization has called repeatedly for Japan to reduce its average workweek further, and we need to assume that average working hours per Japanese will continue to decline. That will complement population decline and demographic aging in diminishing economic growth.

Remarkably, the Japanese government does not appear to have accounted for a shrinking workweek in preparing its long-term economic forecasts. The government has not released any long-term forecasts for economic growth. But we can extrapolate the government's long-term economic assumptions from its projections for the pension program and other projections based on those assumptions. And the numbers suggest that the government forecasters are ignoring the likelihood of a decline in working hours. But they are not alone: a shorter workweek is also conspicuously absent from the assumptions in long-term economic forecasts by some private-sector research organizations.

As seen in figure 9, monthly working hours in Japan display a consistent downward trend over the long term. A sudden leveling of the downward trend line in the graph is implausible. The author has therefore assumed a continuing decline in working hours in preparing the arguments presented in this work.

ONLY TWO-THIRDS AS MUCH LABOR AS BEFORE

Forecasting the decline in average working hours, like forecasting the economically active percentage of the population, is fraught with uncertainty.

Figure 9
Monthly Working Hours in Japan

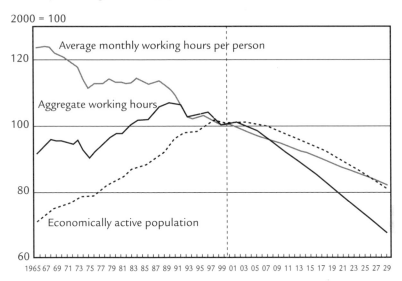

2000 = 100

Average monthly working hours per person

Aggregate working hours

Economically active population

Sources: For the years to 2000, calculations by the author based on labor survey data published by the Statistics Bureau of Japan's Ministry of Internal Affairs and Communications and on monthly labor statistics published by the Ministry of Health, Labor, and Welfare; projections by the author for subsequent years

We can assume that pressure from the International Labor Organization and that other considerations will prompt the government to promote a shorter workweek. But we cannot be equally certain about how aggressively the government will act or about the likely response by corporations and by organized labor.

For lack of a more-convincing scenario, the author has assumed that the past trend in working hours will continue. That assumption underlies the future trend line for monthly working hours in figure 9. The trend is an average annual decline of 0.6% in working hours. That would reduce the average monthly working hours to 126.4 in 2030, from 156.2 in 2000.

Some readers will doubt that Japan's working hours can shrink that much. Even at the assumed pace of decline, Japan would require 20 years to attain the present brevity of Germany's workweek. Japan is thus 20 years behind Germany in this regard, and international opinion is unlikely to countenance that glaring disparity. If anything, we should expect the pace of shrinkage in Japan's workweek to increase.

Multiplying the annual working hours per person by the number of people in the workforce yields a nation's gross annual working hours. The author projects that Japan's gross working hours in 2030 will total 80 billion, down 33.9% from the 2000 total of 121 billion. This is to say that Japan will have only two-thirds as much labor available in 2030 as in 2000. Our task now is to examine what that stunning decline in labor will mean for the Japanese economy.

Japan's Shrinking Economy

Two Kinds of Technological Progress

We saw in chapter 1 that labor productivity and the number of workers determine the size of a nation's gross domestic product (GDP). We also saw that the all-too-rapid shrinking and aging of Japan's population will reduce the number of workers faster than technological progress can raise labor productivity. The labor input in production processes, however, is not the number of workers but the number of worker hours. We will therefore adopt that indicator—characterized simply as labor— in the following discussion.

Another important distinction is between the two kinds of technological progress. One kind of progress consists of automating production processes and thereby reducing the amount of labor required per machine. The other kind of progress consists of increasing the output per machine. Both of these kinds of progress figure in labor productivity. Considering them separately will be useful, however, in examining corporate behavior and in clarifying the relationships of labor and technological progress to GDP.

Raising the ratio of equipment to labor contributes to GDP expansion by increasing the number of units of production per worker. Given a constant amount of labor, raising the capital intensiveness of industry will increase overall production output and spawn economic growth.

Next, let's consider technological progress that raises the efficiency of equipment. That progress can, but does not necessarily, increase capital productivity as measured in units of output per machine. Unlike capital intensiveness, capital productivity is trending downward in the industrial nations. That downward trend reflects increased investment in technologies for reducing the adverse environmental effect of production processes. It also reflects heavy investment in computers and communications equipment in administrative sectors that do not contribute directly to production output.

Also nudging capital productivity downward is the rising cost of raw materials and energy, which tends to diminish production output. In calculating GDP, the figure we use for production output is a net figure: sales minus the cost of raw materials and energy. Raw materials and energy are value-added output for their original suppliers. But for manufacturers of end products, they are costs included in the selling prices of the products. Netting out the cost of raw materials and energy avoids double counting in calculating the aggregate value of production as GDP. The effect of rising raw material or energy costs on capital productivity was dramatically apparent after the oil crises of the 1970s. Capital productivity in the industrialized nations declined markedly in the wake of those events.

So we should not think of progress in improving the efficiency of machines as a means of raising capital productivity; rather, we should regard it as a means of slowing the decline in that indicator. We also need to note, however, a small change in the pattern of the decline in capital productivity in the 1990s. Capital productivity turned upward in the United States, albeit ever so slightly, and it stopped declining and leveled off in Germany and in France. We lack sufficient evidence to judge with confidence whether those developments signal a fundamental change in the long-term trend. What we do know is that capital productivity has continued to decline in Japan. The differences between Japan and the other industrialized nations cited are attributable to problems that Japan faces in research and development capabilities and in production systems. We will take a close look at those problems later in this chapter.

POPULATION DECLINE AND THE DETERMINANTS OF ECONOMIC GROWTH

The decline in Japan's workforce, caused by population shrinkage and aging, reduces the amount of plant and equipment that the nation's economy can support. Plant and equipment require labor to operate, the amount of labor required for each production setup being determined by the applicable technology. The decline in the workforce thus tends to diminish Japan's production capital stock.

Technological progress that reduces the amount of labor required per machine offsets the effect of the declining workforce. Theoretically, progress in automation could completely offset that effect and prevent the diminution of Japan's capital stock. We can regard the level of capital stock as the net result of workforce shrinkage and technological progress. And we can regard GDP as the product of capital stock multiplied by capital productivity.

Improvements in production equipment and in production systems increase the production output per unit of capital stock. They help minimize the decline in capital productivity and thus contribute to economic growth. Conversely, a lack of technological progress for raising equipment efficiency will negate any technological progress for capital productivity through automation.

Capital productivity is trending downward in Japan and is therefore a negative factor in economic growth. Automation is a positive factor in economic growth, but technological development that focuses exclusively on automation and that neglects fundamental improvements in equipment efficiency will fail to raise overall labor productivity—production output per unit of labor. From the perspective of promoting economic growth, we need to emphasize equipment efficiency as well as automation in conducting research and development.

Another way to raise capital productivity is to develop new products of higher value-added. Our concern in this work, however, is with long-term economic trends. An increase in the value-added share of production will raise the long-term economic growth rate only if it is permanent. The new product must offer compelling advantages for which customers are prepared to continue to pay higher prices than before. Only then will it support a lasting rise in capital productivity. Yet, increases in relative value-added achieved through product development tend to be short-lived. Competitors in Japan and in other nations promptly introduce similar products, and price competition soon drives the rate of value-added back down to its original level. The contribution to growth in the Japanese economy is fleeting.

Numerous frivolous products appeared on the market during Japan's bubble economy of the late 1980s. New cars, for example, came loaded with all manner of basically useless accessories. Those products supported high rates of value-added for their manufacturers, but they did not provide value of lasting appeal for consumers. Capital productivity, elevated briefly by the initial surge in sales, returned to its original level when consumers abandoned the products and demand slumped.

THE COMING DECLINE IN CAPITAL STOCK

GDP is born of capital stock, so projecting the level of capital stock is indispensable in forecasting economic growth. As we have seen, the amount of labor available and the pace of automation determine the amount of capital stock that the economy can support. We have already projected trends in the size of Japan's workforce. So if we can develop a sound assumption for the pace of automation, we will have a basis for projecting trends in capital stock.

The rate of technological progress in Japan slowed sharply in the mid-1970s. That happened largely because Japan weaned itself of reliance on technology imports from North America and Europe and began to rely on independent technological development. When Japan was still relying on imported technology, it lagged well behind the West in technological attainment. The imports supported technological leaps—high-paced technological progress that is the privilege of an underdeveloped nation. After Japan caught up with the West technologically, it needed to rely on its own resources—supplemented by occasional imports—for further technological progress. The pace of technological progress in Japan became basically the same as in North America and Europe. And that pace was a lot slower than it had been only a few years earlier.

So we should refer to Japan's rate of technological progress since the late 1970s to identify the pertinent trend. The late 1970s were a chaotic time for the Japanese economy, however, on account of the two oil crises of 1973 and 1979. We will therefore use the average rate of technological progress from the 1980s to 2000 as the basis for our projections.

This approach has its faults. Most notably, the rate of technological progress in the 1980s and 1990s was extremely high in nations worldwide, including Japan. Whether Japan can maintain a comparable rate of technological progress until 2030 is questionable. On the other hand, 30 years is a long time, and important technological breakthroughs could

Figure 10

Capital Stock and Capital Spending in Japan's Private Sector
(not including financial institutions)

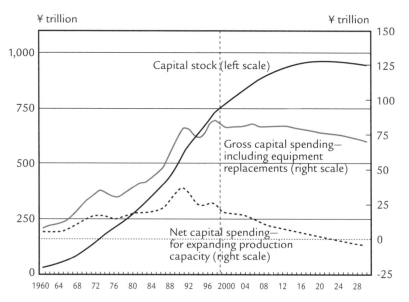

Sources: For the years to 1998, data published by the Economic Planning Agency
(now part of the Cabinet Office) for gross capital spending and net capital spending
and calculations by the author for capital stock; projections by the author for
all items for subsequent years

occur during that time span. So we will use the 1980-to-2000 rate for
our projections, but let us bear in mind that actual technological progress
from 2000 to 2030 will likely be slower than that rate.

Figure 10 presents projections for corporate capital stock, for real
gross investment, and for real net investment based on our assumed rate
of technological progress. The projection for corporate capital stock
excludes capital stock at financial institutions. It indicates continuing
growth until 2021, followed by gradual decline. The decline sets in when
the rising pace of decline in available labor surpasses the rate of technological progress. Japan's capital stock burgeoned 6.7-fold over the 30
years to 2000, but its growth is already slowing dramatically. At its peak
in 2021, the nation's capital stock will total only 20% more than in 2000.

The author has calculated the projections for capital spending in figure 10 on the basis of the projections for corporate capital stock. Here,

gross capital spending comprises investment in new plant and equipment and investment in equipment replacement, and net capital spending excludes investment in equipment replacement. Gross capital spending per year increased 2.8-fold over the 30 years to 2000. The projection for that item in figure 10 shows little change from 2000 to 2006 and then begins a sustained decline. By 2030, it has declined to 88.2% of its 2000 level.

"Investment spawns investment," said people of Japan's postwar economy, and capital spending powered the nation's unprecedented economic growth. Massive capital spending is the reason that Japan consistently outperformed the United States and western European nations in economic growth. That is why we hear calls for stepped-up capital spending to lead Japan out of its present economic malaise. We need to recognize, however, that capital spending in Japan cannot grow over the long term. The nation needs to find a new model for economic growth.

2009: WHEN THE ECONOMY BEGINS TO SHRINK

Let us now forecast Japan's economic growth on the basis of our projections for capital stock. The downward trend in capital productivity means that the economic growth rate will be lower than the growth rate for capital stock. We can therefore assume that economic contraction will accompany a decline in capital stock. An economy, however, consists of the interplay of disparate elements of supply and demand. Economic forecasting needs to include simulations of the manner in which those elements come into balance.

We will employ the growth model of R. F. Harrod and E. D. Dormar, supplemented by the author with an investment constraint. Figure 11 presents forecasts prepared with that model. It represents the economy as national income—net of capital depletion—rather than as GDP.

Here is a simple example of the difference between national income and GDP. Think of an independent taxi driver. The driver earns ¥6 million a year and owns a taxi that costs ¥2 million and that has a useful life of five years. Straight-line depreciation of the vehicle would result in depreciation expense of ¥400,000 a year. GDP ignores that expense and represents the driver's annual income as ¥6 million. National income uses the net figure of ¥5.6 million.

Figure 11

Japanese Real National Income

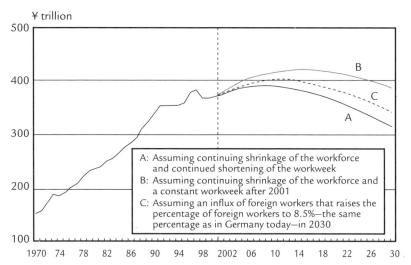

Sources: For the years to 2000, calculations by the author based on Japan's national accounts;
projections by the author for subsequent years

Economic planners prefer national income to GDP as an indicator of living standards, for example, since it consists of income available for people to use. GDP, on the other hand, is the more-useful indicator for handling aggregate corporate sales. Companies are presumably investing in new equipment to replace worn-out equipment, and that investment offsets the capital depletion component of GDP. And for companies that produce capital goods, whether customers use their products as replacement items or as new production capacity is irrelevant, the sales value is the same.

Although national income is smaller than GDP, the two move almost exactly in parallel. An increase or decrease in national income means a nearly identical change in GDP. So national income is, for our purposes, interchangeable with GDP as a measure of economic growth.

Forecast A in figure 11 suggests that Japan's economy will begin to contract in 2009. The economy grew rapidly for decades, and Japan's national income in 2000 was ¥370.3 trillion. Forecast A indicates that the national income will continue growing until 2008, when it will reach ¥390.7 trillion, and that it will then begin contracting, shrinking to ¥314.6

trillion by 2030. That would be a decline of 15.0% from 2000. The annual rate of economic contraction indicated by forecast A, 0.2% in 2010, escalates to 1.1% in 2020 and to 1.7% in 2030. This is an unmistakable picture of persistent and accelerating economic decline.

Recall that we have employed an optimistic assumption for the pace of technological progress. Yet the resultant forecasts still depict a deepening decline. The shrinkage and aging of Japan's population are simply proceeding too rapidly to be offset through any conceivable amount of technological progress.

THE INEVITABILITY OF ECONOMIC CONTRACTION

Note that figure 11 contains two scenarios in addition to forecast A. In forecast B, the author has eliminated the decrease in working hours per person assumed in forecast A. A sudden halt to the long-standing downward trend in working hours seems highly unlikely, as noted earlier. But as also noted, several economic forecasters assume a constant workweek in their calculations, so the author has included forecast B for the sake of comparison.

With a constant workweek, the Japanese economy continues growing for a little longer than in forecast A—until 2014—but it then descends into the same basic downward pattern. National income grows at an average annual rate of 0.9% from 2000 to 2014, but it is declining 0.4% a year by 2020 and 0.9% a year by 2030.

Forecast C in figure 11 addresses the oft-heard calls for employing foreign workers to maintain Japan's economic growth momentum. The author has assumed an infusion of foreign labor in calculating forecast C. Of the largest industrialized nations, Germany has the highest percentage of foreign workers in its workforce. Foreign residents account for fully 8.5% of Germany's population. Forecast C incorporates the assumption that Japan encourages an influx of foreign workers and that the percentage of those workers in the nation's workforce increases steadily and reaches the present German level in 2030.

In this scenario, Japan's national income peaks in 2013 and then enters the same basic pattern of decline seen in forecasts A and B. National income's average annual growth rate from 2000 to 2013 is 0.6%, and its annual rate of contraction reaches 0.8% in 2020 and 1.5% in 2030.

Figure 11 thus demonstrates that neither a constant workweek nor an influx of foreign workers can forestall the coming economic contraction significantly. Economic effectiveness aside, both of those supposed countermeasures entail problems that cast doubt on their viability.

A shorter workweek is an important benefit of economic progress. Economic growth, industrial specialization, and productivity gains have freed people from long working hours and given them time to spend at their discretion. That has enabled people to indulge wide-ranging interests and to foster a diversity of communities. Free time is essential to the richer, more-fulfilling lifestyles that Japanese have begun to pursue in earnest. Aborting the ongoing trend toward a shorter workweek would sacrifice that benefit without achieving the ostensible aim of preventing economic contraction. The shrinkage and aging of Japanese society will impose that contraction regardless of any reasonably conceivable development in average working hours. Note that the reduction in working hours is the result of gains in labor productivity and that it therefore includes an implicit increase in hourly compensation.

Welcoming an influx of foreign workers, meanwhile, simply foists onto future generations the economic problems associated with demographic change. That countermeasure only delays the economic switch over from growth to contraction by five years. Yet it obliges future generations to cope with problems of population shrinkage and aging that they would not need to face otherwise. In any case, population shrinkage and aging are not problems that Japan can realistically hope to resolve with foreign workers. Japan would need to host some 24 million foreign workers in 2030 to maintain its workforce at its present size. Those workers would then account for more than 20% of the working population—a clearly untenable proportion.

Corporations in Japan will struggle to cope with the new reality of economic contraction. Japan's economic system rests on the premise of continuing economic growth based on continuing growth in population and in labor, and economic contraction renders important elements of Japanese management methodology obsolete. However, ignoring demographics and macroeconomic reality in the name of preserving or minimizing the change required in familiar management methods is shortsighted and dangerous.

Downsizing Is Crucial to Corporate Management

THE DIFFERENCE IN ECONOMIC MECHANISMS BETWEEN AN EXPANDING POPULATION AND A SHRINKING POPULATION

In this section, we will examine what trends in Japan's working population and in the Japanese economy mean for corporate management. We will begin by examining the difference in economic mechanisms between an expanding population and a shrinking population.

Economic demand comprises personal consumption, housing investment, capital spending, fiscal expenditures, and exports. Demand trends upward in an economy where a growing population spawns an expanding supply of labor, and nearly all of the demand depends on personal incomes in that economy. The funding for personal consumption and for housing investment is wages and salaries. Capital spending also depends on personal incomes, at least to the extent that it is for producing consumer goods. Fiscal expenditures, too, depend on personal incomes for funding. Individuals contribute part of their incomes directly to government revenues through personal income taxes. Meanwhile, companies pay corporate income taxes and sales tax with revenues from sales to consumers, so those tax payments also depend on personal incomes.

Exports are the only element of demand that doesn't depend on wages and salaries in the local economy; they depend on wages and salaries in the importing nations. More precisely, net exports—exports minus imports—are demand in the Japanese economy funded with wages and salaries in the exports' destination markets. Imports are demand in the overseas economies funded with Japanese wages and salaries.

Japan's net exports are extremely small as a percentage of the overall economy; they averaged 1.5% over the years from 1970 to 2000. So we can regard demand as basically equal to the sum of all wages and salaries in the economy. When labor is in a growth mode, total wages and salaries also grow, and demand thus grows, too. When labor is in a negative-growth mode, total wages and salaries decline, as does demand.

Total demand is equal to GDP. We discussed the forecasts for the Japanese economy mainly in terms of production; that is, supply. No

Figure 12

Japanese Production Capacity in Comparison with Labor and Demand

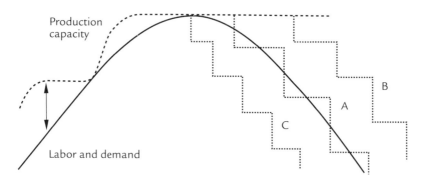

company, however, manufactures products for long that it cannot sell. So supply and demand are simply two different ways of looking at the size of the GDP. A decline in total wages and salaries caused by a decline in available labor diminishes demand and causes the economy to contract. And that is what is about to happen in Japan.

Figure 12 shows supply and demand in an economy of expanding population and in an economy of shrinking population. In a real economy, small differences arise between the short-term movements in labor and demand. Both labor and demand basically move in the same direction, however, so the author has plotted them on the same lines for the sake of simplicity. That is, the line for total working hours in figure 9 (page 27) and the line for national income in forecast A in figure 11 (page 34) appear as the same line in figure 12. Labor and demand in Japan have hitherto moved steadily upward. Now, they will move steadily downward. The resultant curve traces a mountain peak, and Japan's economy is near the summit of that peak.

The dotted line in figure 12 represents the productive capacity of plant and equipment in Japan. This is the amount of production that would be possible if the plant and equipment operated at full capacity. That amount thus differs from actual production and from demand.

In Japanese corporate management, capital spending behavior has centered on expanding production capacity continually to meet future growth in demand. Periods of especially vigorous capital spending have raised Japan's production capacity above the level of demand and created temporary gaps in supply and demand, also known as deflation gaps. The vertical two-way arrow on the left side of the mountain peak in figure 12 illustrates one of those gaps.

An excess of supply over demand means that some plant and equipment is idle. It does not remain idle for long, however, in an economy of expanding population. Corporations simply refrain from additional investment—the horizontal portions of the dotted line—until growing demand catches up with production capacity, and they then put the formerly idle plant and equipment to work. This sequence plays out consistently because expanding labor spawns growth in demand and simultaneously supports growth in production capacity. The growth trend in total wages and salaries spawns continuing growth in demand. Consequently, the growth in production capacity does not cause a lasting increase in idle plant and equipment.

Everything changes in an economy of shrinking population. Even if corporations refrain from new investment and simply maintain their production capacity at a constant level—the dotted line to the right of the mountain-peak curve in figure 12—the declining trend in demand will cause a continuing increase in idle plant and equipment. The supply-and-demand gap will broaden annually, as seen in the broadening distance between the dotted line and the solid line in the right half of figure 12. In addition, the declining availability of labor will reduce the amount of plant and equipment that is even potentially operable, and that will add further to the pool of idle plant and equipment. Production capacity in an economy of shrinking population thus needs to decline in step with the declines in demand and in labor.

THE NEED FOR REDUCING PRODUCTION CAPACITY SYSTEMATICALLY

Let us take a closer look at what a shrinking population implies for corporate management. Let's assume that the solid line in figure 12 represents the labor at a single company and that it also represents the demand for that company's goods. The company's profitability deteriorates when the supply-and-demand gap on the left side of the mountain-peak curve broadens. The left side of figure 12 denotes an expanding-population economy, however, so management can count on upward-trending demand to support a subsequent improvement in the company's cash flow position.

The company's profitability is strongest when production capacity matches demand exactly. But capital spending typically entails long lead times, so management gladly accepts some amount of surplus production capacity in anticipation of future growth in demand.

Maintaining surplus production capacity can be fatal, however, in a contracting-population economy. The supply-and-demand gap broadens at an accelerating pace. That undermines the company's profitability and, in the absence of countermeasures, drives the company into bankruptcy. To avoid that fate, management needs to determine the future levels of labor and demand and reduce production capacity accordingly.

Line A in figure 12 represents a stepwise reduction in production capacity matched to the declines in labor and demand. Although the declines in labor and demand trace a smoothly curving path, companies ordinarily reduce production capacity in block-like increments. They might take a large machine out of operation, shut down a production line, or close a plant.

The very notion of reducing production capacity has been anathema to Japanese management. Only in unfortunate industrial sectors subject to structural decline—such as coal mining and textile manufacturing—have Japanese manufacturers reduced production capacity systematically. But in the shrinking-population economy, reducing production capacity will become common behavior for companies in every sector. It will be essential to corporate survival.

Companies have different ways of reducing production capacity. The most-obvious way, of course, is to turn off and dispose of equipment in operation. A gentler approach is to reduce capacity through attrition: don't replace equipment that reaches the end of its useful life. This approach has the additional benefit of minimizing waste and maximizing profitability, but it requires fastidious planning in capital spending.

The company needs to schedule investment to adapt production capacity to the declining curve—labor and demand—in the right half of figure 12. That means giving careful consideration to the useful life of equipment in making investment decisions. Whereas production equipment typically has a long useful life of 10 years or so, labor and demand will be declining rapidly in Japan's shrinking-population economy. So corporate management will need to devote careful attention to this issue.

MOUNTING RISK IN CAPITAL SPENDING

Line B in figure 12 shows what can happen if management fails to reduce production capacity in step with the declines in labor and demand. The gap between line B and the solid line denotes the losses the company incurs by overestimating labor and demand in its investment planning. Note that losses increase annually.

Overly pessimistic estimates of labor and demand can also be costly. Line C in figure 12 shows what can happen if a company fails to secure production capacity commensurate with the amount of available labor and with the level of demand. That failure does not burden the company with idle plant and equipment, and it does not diminish profitability. But it results in the opportunity cost of lost sales. And like the losses that result from excess production capacity, that opportunity cost increases annually.

Japan's expanding-population economy rewarded companies for intuitively aggressive capital spending. Its shrinking-population economy will require companies to adopt more-scientific approaches to investment planning. The risks inherent in capital spending will increase dramatically. Failure to gauge labor and demand accurately will have unprecedented repercussions for corporate performance. Nor will managements be able to count on the passage of time to rectify their errors; time will amplify the adverse effects of inaccuracy in investment planning.

Even the best managements will be unable to gauge labor and demand with consistent accuracy. Companies will need to hedge against inaccuracies by aiming for the higher rates of return and by accumulating ample reservoirs of retained earnings. They will also need to change the ways they finance their capital spending. The mounting risk associated with capital spending makes bank borrowings, which require annual interest payments, an unsuitable financing option. Instead, companies will need to rely increasingly on equity financing, where the cost of capital is contingent on the companies' success.

What bears repeating here is that the dominant theme in capital spending for all companies will be downscaling. Some companies will post sales growth for a while even amid Japan's economic contraction, but the overall decline in demand will make sales growth unsustainable over the long term. Skillful downsizing will be essential to maintaining corporate vitality. Some American managements have even gone so far as to disband companies that slip below specified criteria for profitability, and that is presumably an option in Japan, too. It would entail huge write-offs, however, since the average life of production equipment, as noted, is about 10 years. That approach would only be appealing in the presence of highly profitable investment alternatives. And such opportunities will be rare in Japan's shrinking-population economy.

THE NONSOLUTION OF CURTAILING WAGES AND SALARIES

From a national perspective, curtailing wages and salaries is the wrong way to raise profitability and increase retained earnings. Total wages and salaries determine the level of demand, so curtailing them triggers a vicious circle. Lowering wages and salaries is likely to depress demand below the level assumed in investment planning. That would oblige companies to further cut back their capital spending or even to shut down more plant and equipment. Since capital spending is an important component of aggregated demand, that would oblige companies to reduce production capacity even further. Economists call this vicious circle a downward cumulative process. But the more common expression, deflationary spiral, is a suitably compelling description.

Japan has experienced deflationary spirals twice in recent history, but both instances occurred while the population was growing. Consequently, the downward spirals were largely a matter of declining growth rates, not sharp and absolute declines, in personal consumption and in capital spending. Japan's first deflationary spiral occurred in the 1970s, after the first oil crisis. The second occurred in the latter half of the 1990s. In both instances, wage and salary curtailment was a principal factor.

Industry curtailed wages and salaries in the 1970s under a government-led program of suppressing aggregate demand. Total wages and salaries declined after the mid-1990s as a result of corporate restructuring and reductions in wage and salary levels. From a narrow perspective, curtailing wages and salaries might seem a good way to bolster corporate profitability, to increase retained earnings, and—in the instance of the 1990s—to secure the financial wherewithal to write off bad loans. But managements need to recognize that curtailing wages and salaries is a self-defeating tactic.

Some readers might object that declining wages and salaries are simply a result, not a cause, of slowing economic growth. The author is referring here, however, to reductions in wages and salaries larger than anything explainable in the framework of an autonomous economic mechanism. The artificially induced reductions in the two examples were part of a uniquely Japanese mechanism. Companies reacted to weakening profitability by lowering wages and salaries even more than the natural decline, and that caused an unnecessarily severe softening of demand.

Figure 13 shows how well wage and salary levels followed gains in labor productivity in different industrialized nations. A value of 100% means that a percentage increase in labor productivity was accompanied by a rise in the wages and salaries of an identical percentage. If an autonomous economic mechanism were the sole determinant of wages and salaries, we would expect the percentage movement in wages and salaries to match the movement in labor productivity exactly. Wage and salary levels, to be sure, are subject to the artificiality of negotiations between labor and management. But we can regard their movement as basically consistent with an autonomous economic mechanism if it is between 50% and 150% of the movement in labor productivity.

GDP, as we have seen, is the product of labor multiplied by labor productivity, and total wages and salaries determine consumption. When wages and salaries rise less than labor productivity, consumption declines as a percentage of GDP, and the economy grows more slowly than previously or even contracts.

Wages and salaries have underperformed labor productivity substantially more in Japan than in other industrialized nations almost throughout the period covered by figure 13. That underperformance is especially pronounced from the latter half of the 1970s to the former half of the 1980s and in the latter half of the 1990s. It was worst in the mid-1980s, when wages and salaries barely rose at all while productivity was rising 2% to 4% annually. That all but forces us to conclude that wages and salaries were subject to artificial restraints.

Twice in the recent past, wages and salaries thus appear to have come under massive and artificial downward pressure. And the result in both of those instances was a deflationary spiral. We should know from that experience that artificially suppressing wages and salaries enervates demand and ultimately undercuts corporate profitability.

Figure 13

Movement in Wage and Salary Levels in Comparison with Gains in
Labor Productivity

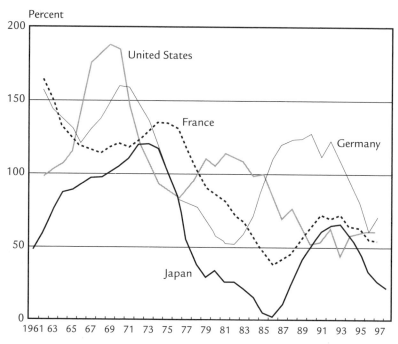

Note: The figures for labor productivity and for wage and salary levels are per hour worked

Source: Calculations by the author based on annual national accounts data
published by the OECD

In a shrinking-population economy, demand trends downward, corporate sales revenues decline, and corporate profits drop in absolute terms
even if companies can maintain their profit margins. Ill-considered measures to buttress corporate profitability by curtailing wages and salaries
worsen the earnings environment. They summon to mind a familiar
Japanese proverb about the hungry octopus that eats its own legs.

Economic policy needs to focus not on corporate earnings but on the
sum of corporate earnings and wages and salaries, which is industry's
value-added, and on value-added as a percentage of corporate sales revenues. That focus will help maintain wages and salaries at the appropriate level and, ultimately, will help secure sound profitability for
corporations.

Japanese corporations remain far behind their North American and European counterparts in maximizing value-added as a percentage of sales, and the gap is broadening. Raising the value-added rate should be a top priority for Japanese business as it enters the era of a shrinking-population economy. We will return to this subject.

THE DIFFERENT ECONOMIC BENEFITS OF WAGES AND SALARIES AND OF CORPORATE PROFITS

The preceding text has emphasized the importance of wages and salaries in demand. Some readers will note, however, that corporate purchasing is also a big part of demand and will question why we should care about the balance between wages and salaries and corporate profits in total value-added. We should care about the balance because rising wages and salaries and rising corporate profits have strikingly different economic benefits. That difference becomes especially profound in a shrinking-population economy. The reason lies in the reductions that will be under way in capital spending.

We saw in figure 12 (page 38) that corporations will need to reduce their production capacity. That scaling back will necessarily include reductions in capital spending. In figure 10 (page 32), we saw forecasts for gross capital spending and for net capital spending. Those forecasts indicate that net capital spending will enter a sustained decline in 2022. That decline is highly significant in regard to the question at hand.

Companies retain a portion of their earnings to fund investment in new production capacity. Economists refer to that practice as corporate accumulation. It corresponds to consumers accumulating savings for down payments on home purchases. Separately, corporations accumulate a portion of income as depreciation to pay for replacing worn-out equipment. Companies account for depreciation as an expense charged against taxable income, not as a distribution of earnings, so accumulated depreciation is reliably available for purchases of replacement equipment. Reducing production capacity will mean retaining a smaller amount of earnings for investment in new production capacity. It will also mean that depreciation will begin to exceed the amount required for replacing equipment.

The decline in net capital spending—investment in new production capacity—will thus reduce the importance of retained earnings. Companies will retain earnings mainly just to hedge against investment risk and against possible business downturns. Reducing the proportion of corporate value-added that companies allocate to wages and salaries (labor distribution in economics lingo) will cause a comparable increase in retained earnings (corporate accumulation). But in a shrinking-population economy, companies will have no means of employing the retained earnings productively. Lending to other companies—principally through banks and other intermediaries—has been a traditional means of employing excess retained earnings, but corporate Japan will have an aggregate excess of retained earnings. The supply of funds will exceed demand. An economy where the corporate sector has an aggregate excess of retained earnings, known as savings excess, is a shrinking economy.

ECONOMIC CONTRACTION CAUSED BY SAVINGS EXCESS

Here is what needs to happen for companies in Japan to sell the same amount of goods next month that they sold this month: All of this month's sales revenues need to reach consumers and companies as wages and salaries, as payments for parts and raw materials, and—through banks and other intermediaries—as lending. That way, customers—consumers and companies—will have enough funds to purchase the same amount of goods next month.

Accumulation excess means that a portion of this month's sales revenues will not reach the prospective customers for next month's sales. Less money will be available for purchases, and sales will decline. In other words, the economy will contract. Curtailing wages and salaries depresses economic growth by generating this kind of savings excess. It would cause Japan's impending economic contraction to be even greater than the author has forecasted in this work.

Companies can avoid savings excess and its attendant economic demerits by increasing their dividend payments, as well as by raising wages and salaries. Dividends also raise personal incomes and thus strengthen purchasing power. But dividends differ somewhat from wages and salaries in their economic benefits. That's because the recipients of dividend payments—shareholders—tend to be individuals of higher-than-average incomes. High-income individuals spend a lower percentage of incremental income on consumption than do individuals who have lower incomes. Increasing dividend payments is therefore less effective than raising wages and salaries in stimulating economic growth.

We have seen that Japan entered a deflationary spiral in the latter half of the 1990s. That deflationary spiral resulted from allocating liquidity inefficiently. An economy expands and contracts to adjust national savings—the sum of personal, corporate, and government savings, where the government portion includes pension savings—to gross investment, which involves capital spending, public works spending, housing investment, and net exports. That expansion and contraction takes place through an autonomous mechanism known as the savings-investment balance. If savings exceed investment, the economy contracts. Income levels then decline until people can save only as much as is being invested.

Investment declines in a shrinking-population economy, so the danger of a savings surplus is great. Allocating value-added appropriately between wages and salaries and corporate earnings is especially important in forestalling that danger.

THE DIFFERENCE BETWEEN A RECESSION AND A SHRINKING-POPULATION ECONOMY

A shrinking-population economy resembles in some ways a continuing series of recessions. That has prompted some people to mistakenly conclude that a shrinking-population economy makes deterioration in companies' financial position inevitable. To be sure, corporate sales revenues decline in a shrinking-population economy, like they do in a recession. But that needn't result in a recession-like deterioration in companies' financial position.

Economic contraction in a shrinking-population economy begins on the supply side; a recessionary contraction begins on the demand side. Corporate performance deteriorates in a recession because companies are unable to secure demand commensurate with production capacity. The possible reasons for a downturn in demand are multifarious: a spike in prices for goods caused by an energy crunch, ill-conceived efforts to curtail wages and earnings, the end of a consumption or investment boom, and any of numerous other events.

Whatever the reason for the weakening of demand, inventories pile up and sap companies' liquidity. Companies reduce production to pare inventories back to sound levels, capacity utilization rates decline, and companies experience difficulty in servicing the debt that they incurred to purchase plant and equipment. As the reduced purchasing of raw materials aggravates the worsening economic picture, demand slumps throughout the economy.

The troubles for a shrinking-population economy, in contrast, begin with a decline in production capacity caused by a labor shortage. Rather than encountering a slump in demand, companies experience a slump in their ability to produce goods, and their sales decline accordingly. A shrinking-population economy presents daunting issues for companies and for the nation as a whole. But those problems are surmountable through wise economic policy and sound corporate management.

Inflation caused by an excess of demand over supply capacity is unthinkable. Nor will companies need to cope with overcapacity and resultant unsold goods, as long as wages and salaries are at appropriate levels. Meanwhile, companies can avoid the problem of idle plant and equipment by reducing production capacity in step with the decline in labor. That will enable them to avoid the burden of paying interest on loans for plant and equipment not actually in use.

Our operative principle here is "surmountable." Companies can surmount the issues posed by a shrinking-population economy, but only through sound, collective management policy and determined, well-focused effort. To repeat, wages and salaries need to be at appropriate levels, and companies need to reduce their production capacity at a suitable pace. Wage and salary levels and capacity utilization are issues in a growing-population economy, too, and perhaps do not warrant special mention here. But as we have seen, Japan has twice suffered the unhappy results of artificially constraining wages and salaries in recent history. And experience suggests that maintaining plant and equipment at suitable levels is more difficult than it might sound. So the author has seen fit to emphasize both of these issues in connection with a shrinking-population economy, where the penalty for missteps is even more severe.

DOWNSIZING TO WIN

Maximizing sales has long been the top management priority for Japanese companies. Japanese have tended to rate companies primarily on the basis of sales volume and percentage sales growth. That is in contrast with

North Americans and Europeans, who have focused more on earnings and on profit margins. Japan's shrinking labor pool and declining demand mandate a change in priorities. Downsizing skillfully will become a prerequisite for competitiveness and vitality in Japanese industry.

Companies that seek to increase profits by cutting wages and salaries below appropriate levels will damage the economy, as well as cut their own throats. Managements should learn from past experience and recognize that artificially curtailing wages and salaries undercuts demand and ultimately depresses sales and profits. Everyone needs to recognize that a deflationary spiral in a shrinking-population economy would be far more severe and prolonged than a comparable spiral in a growing-population economy.

In a growing-population economy, the upward trend in demand eventually catches up with excess production capacity and lifts the economy out of its deflationary spiral. Demand trends downward, however, in a shrinking-population economy. Escaping from a deflationary spiral would depend on reducing production capacity even faster than the decline in demand. Companies would need to shut down plant and equipment ruthlessly. Company after company would go under.

Automation as a Nonsolution

Japan's Failure with Obsessive Automation

Automation strikes many in Japanese industry as a solution to the problem of a shrinking labor pool. Some have even suggested that automation will become the prime focus of Japanese capital spending. However, the author has factored progress in automation into the economic forecasts presented in this work. The assumption here is of technological progress in automation at the average rate that has prevailed since the 1980s. Only progress substantially in excess of that assumed rate would change the economic outlook significantly.

A more-pertinent question is whether wholesale automation is good medicine for the Japanese economy. In examining that question, we need to begin by reviewing previous investment in automation and its results. Figure 14 presents year-on-year growth in capital intensiveness as a result

Figure 14

Marginal Productivity of Capital and Year-on-Year Growth in
Capital Intensiveness

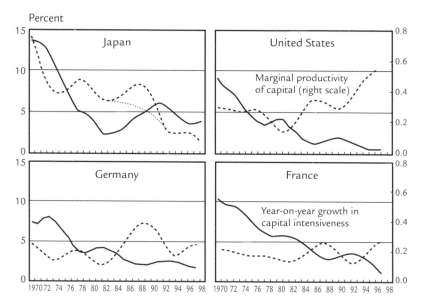

Sources: Corporate reports and calculations by the author based on
annual national accounts data published by the OECD

of automation investment in Japan, the United States, Germany, and
France. The United States, Germany, and France show a steadily downward trend, but Japan shows a markedly different pattern. Japan's annual growth rate in capital intensiveness declined sharply in the 1970s but
rebounded strongly in the early 1980s. Although the rate declined somewhat after the collapse of the bubble economy of the 1980s, it has
remained a great deal higher than in other industrialized nations.

Companies in other nations also invested heavily in automation in
the past, but they later lost some of their enthusiasm for automating production. Japan alone has been investing aggressively in automation since
the early 1980s. That investment has taken place amid an overall increase
in capital intensiveness, so it has redoubled the pace of computerization
and mechanization in Japanese industry. Japan's veritably obsessive investment in automation has filled factories throughout the nation with robots
and with other kinds of ostensibly laborsaving equipment. By the beginning

of the 1990s, Japan was home to some 60% of the industrial robots in operation worldwide.

Japan's obsessive automation, however, has been less than successful. The dotted line for marginal productivity in figure 14 traces the disappointing results. Marginal productivity is an indicator of return on capital spending. Economists calculate marginal productivity by dividing the increase in production value-added by the increase in capital stock (investment in new production capacity). A low figure for marginal productivity indicates that capital spending has been inefficient and even wasteful. Note, however, that the value-added in the calculation of marginal productivity includes salaries and wages, as well as corporate profits.

Marginal production in Japan shows a precipitous downward trend since the early 1980s (figure 14). The trend would be straight downward but for an upturn during Japan's bubble economy. In figure 14, the thin dotted line shows the trend in marginal productivity net of the effects of the economic bubble. In none of the other three nations represented does marginal productivity decline so markedly. The decline in Japan's marginal productivity is attributable to obsessive investment in automation, which appears to have yielded extremely low return on investment. We will return to this subject.

Defenders of automation investment could note that Japan's economy has been in prolonged stagnation, interrupted only by the bubble economy. They could argue that the decline in marginal productivity is attributable to that stagnation, not to investment in automation. The author, however, has adjusted for capacity utilization in calculating the capital stock figures used in figure 14. That adjustment has eliminated any idle plant and equipment attributable to weak sales. So economic stagnation is not a factor in the decline in marginal productivity portrayed in the figure.

JAPANESE COMPANIES' RESPONSE TO THE SHRINKING POOL OF CORE LABOR

Figure 15 reveals a possible reason for Japanese companies' continuing obsession with automation despite the daunting decline in marginal productivity. It shows the declining availability of labor in the 20-to-39 age range—the core of the workforce—and the increasing employment of

Figure 15

Left Graph:
Year-on-Year Change in Japan's Male and Female Population Aged 20 to 39 and in Japan's Female Population Aged 40 to 54
Right Graph:
The Correspondence of Japanese Wages and Salaries to Gains in Labor Productivity and the Economically Active Percentage of Japanese Women Aged 40 to 54

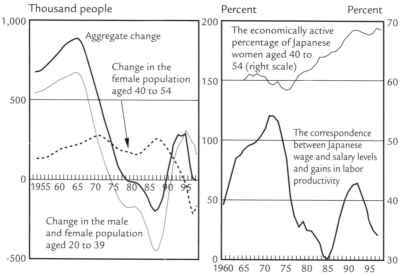

Source: Calculations by the author based on census data, labor survey data, and national accounts data

middle-aged women. The inevitable aging of Japanese society was a foregone conclusion by the early 1960s. But that demographic change did not begin to affect the labor supply until 1968. In that year, population growth in the 20-to-39 age range slowed for the first time in the postwar era. And in 1976, the population in that age range began to decline. Japanese industry responded to the new difficulty of securing labor in that age range by increasing the employment of middle-aged women. The economically active percentage of Japanese women aged 40 to 54 increased rapidly, starting in 1976.

Japan's aging proceeded extremely fast, however, and in 1980 the aggregate population of males and females aged 20 to 39 and of women aged 40 to 54 began to decline. A rising percentage of economically active

Japanese prevented a decline in the number of workers in those demographic groups, but the labor market was growing inexorably tighter. A growing pool of labor had been fundamental to the continuing postwar growth in Japanese production. The tightening supply and demand for labor exposed the impending limits to that pattern, and industry responded by automating production extensively.

Employing large numbers of middle-aged women, incidentally, had bolstered profitability for Japanese companies. Most of the working women aged 40 to 54 held low-wage part-time jobs. The growing percentage of middle-aged women in the workforce thus lowered the average wage and salary levels. That is evident in the right graph in figure 15. The upper line shows the economically active percentage of women aged 40 to 54. Beneath it is the line from figure 13 (page 44) for the correspondence of wages and salaries to gains in labor productivity. That correspondence turned negative in 1976, when the economically active percentage of women aged 40 to 54 began to rise, and it subsequently continued to plunge. We have seen that Japan exercised artificial constraint on wages and salaries in the 1970s, and increasing the percentage of low-paid middle-aged women in the workforce was an important part of that policy. That was in addition to restraining wage and salary gains for the existing workforce.

Corporate profits are what's left of production value-added after subtracting wages and salaries. So keeping wage and salary growth inappropriately low—lower than the pace of gains in labor productivity—enabled companies to secure excessive profits. Companies then began investing heavily in automation in the early 1980s to maintain production levels amid a dwindling supply of core labor. Unnaturally low wage and salary levels offset the resultant decline in the value-added percentage of sales and enabled companies to secure larger profits than the market mechanism would normally permit. Managements were counting on this stratagem to keep their companies afloat.

A SEVERE DETERIORATION IN CORPORATE BALANCE SHEETS

Japanese companies' survival-and-growth stratagem soured in the 1990s. Massive investment in automation drove marginal productivity down almost to nothing. Managements had sought to maintain profitability by constraining wages and salaries. But the sum of their profits and their employees' wages and salaries—production value-added—all but ceased growing. Meanwhile, corporate balance sheets deteriorated under a swelling burden of debt undertaken to finance the automation investment.

Overinvestment in automation in the 1980s must share the blame with the bubble economy for the bad-debt malaise that afflicted Japan in the 1990s. This is not to suggest that all companies invested unwisely. But from a macroeconomic perspective, Japanese industry as a whole made a wrong turn. The errors of the many more than negated the prudence of the few.

Investment in automation need not have caused the decline in marginal productivity that we see in figure 14 (page 50). Companies could have avoided that pitfall if they had been less obsessed with maintaining and even expanding production and if they had abided by a more-gradual approach to automation. Production output naturally reflects the expansion and contraction of the workforce. Automation investment oriented toward raising return on investment would have benefited the companies and their workers.

The inevitability of prolonged shrinkage in Japan's workforce was more than evident at the outset of the 1980s. Profound change was already under way in the production environment. Oblivious to that change, Japanese companies cast aside considerations of return on investment and invested massively in automation in the futile hope of maintaining production output at historic levels. The futility of that exercise is now clear for all the world to see.

OVERINVESTMENT IN AUTOMATION AS AN ECONOMIC ALBATROSS

In figure 16, the author has evaluated capital spending in principal industrialized nations. This evaluation is on the basis of the growth theory of the American economist Robert Solow. The value of zero on the vertical axis indicates maximal return on investment; that is, a maximal increase in value-added per unit of capital spending. A value higher than zero indicates excessive investment in relation to the amount of available labor, a value lower than zero, insufficient investment. Excessive investment and insufficient investment both cause return on investment to be lower than it would be otherwise.

Figure 16

Sufficiency of Capital Spending in Principal Industrialized Nations

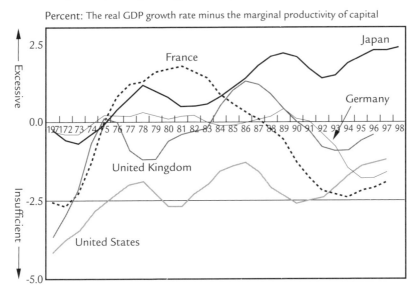

Source: Calculations by the author based on annual national accounts data
published by the OECD

We have noted that Japan's marginal productivity would not have declined so sharply if automation investment had transpired at an appropriate level—a level that would have supported rising return on investment. In figure 16, that level would be around zero on the vertical axis. And since aggregate value-added is national income, a value of zero on that axis denotes maximal economic growth. Values higher or lower than zero indicate sacrifices in the growth rate.

The nation that displays the most-optimal level of capital spending in our comparison is the Federal Republic of Germany before the east-west reunification. Germany's capital spending became insufficient, according to figure 16, amid the special circumstances of coping with reunification in the early 1990s. But Germany later redressed that insufficiency.

The next-best performer in our comparison is the United Kingdom. Capital spending in the United States, meanwhile, has traditionally been lower than the optimal level. But an improvement in U.S. investment performance is evident over the long term, and the United States came close to overcoming its insufficiency in capital spending in the 1990s. France's investment performance has fluctuated widely, but France also displays a convergence toward optimal investment over the long term.

The delinquent in our comparison is Japan. To be sure, our reading of figure 16 needs to allow for such mitigating factors as cyclical economic trends and statistical error. But even discounting those factors, Japan's capital spending had become unmistakably excessive by the early 1980s, and the magnitude of Japan's overinvestment has since trended relentlessly upward.

No other nation has displayed such manic investment behavior as Japan. And the bulk of Japan's capital spending has consisted of investment in automation. That investment includes automated systems adopted by manufacturers in their efforts to expand production capacity in a tight labor market. But whatever the purpose of the investment, increasingly excessive capital spending commands attention as a possible cause of Japan's prolonged economic stagnation in recent years.

AUTOMATION AIMED AT OPTIMAL CAPITAL INTENSIVENESS

The preceding condemnation of investment in automation is somewhat counterintuitive. After all, automation presumably raises labor productivity and increases sales. So the reader is to be forgiven for questioning why Japan's investment in automation should have retarded economic growth.

Figure 17 helps explain where Japanese capital spending went wrong. The horizontal axis in the graph represents capital intensiveness. Capital intensiveness rises to the right and declines to the left. Higher capital intensiveness means higher labor productivity, which means greater output, as indicated by the thick curve in the graph. Investment in automation, however, raises the cost of production. The cost of production rises in direct proportion to the increase in the amount of equipment employed, so that rise appears in the graph as a climbing straight line. The dotted line in the graph is value-added. That is what remains after subtracting the cost of production from production output.

What strikes us immediately in figure 17 is the contrasting patterns in production output and production cost. Rising capital intensiveness entails a straight-line increase in cost but yields diminishing gains in production output. Value-added rises markedly in the early stages of automation

Figure 17

The Relationship between Capital Intensiveness and Production
Output, Production Cost, and Value-Added

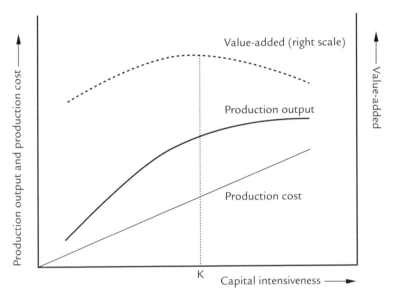

investment. But value-added begins to decline when progressive automation pushes capital intensiveness beyond the threshold indicated as K in figure 17.

The rise and subsequent decline in production output is a phenomenon commonly observed in the real economy. That phenomenon demonstrates what economists call the law of diminishing marginal productivity. In short, increases in capital intensiveness cannot support identical percentage increases in production output indefinitely. That's because human labor remains more productive than robots and other equipment in some phases of production. A combination of human labor and automated equipment is ordinarily the best way to maximize overall efficiency in manufacturing.

Processes where humans frequently retain a productivity edge in some phases of work include the loading of raw materials, inventory management, product assembly, inter-process conveyance, inspection, and shipping. Highly skilled labor, especially, remains indispensable in numerous crucial functions. Automated equipment is far more accurate and efficient than humans, of course, in work that presents demanding tolerances. A good example is the fabrication of semiconductor devices. But robotic sensors and arms remain inferior to the eyes and hands of skilled humans in a vast range of assembly work. And the human touch frequently remains essential in moving items efficiently from one process to the next.

Figure 17 reinforces the message that excessive investment in automation can depress a nation's economic growth rate. Value-added and economic growth are highest at the threshold, K. If a large number of manufacturers pass that threshold and operate at excessive levels of capital intensiveness, the nation's economic growth rate will suffer. The shapes of the curves in figure 17 vary by industrial sector and by mode of business, and the level of capital intensiveness that maximizes value-added varies by product. But every company has an optimal level of capital intensiveness, of automation. Undertaking optimal automation at each company in a nation is an effective way to maximize the nation's economic growth rate. That corporate behavior brings a nation toward the ideal value of zero on the vertical axis in figure 16. Rational approaches to automation by companies are why the United States is trending toward zero and why Germany, the United Kingdom, and France are converging around that value.

Japanese companies also displayed rational approaches to automation until the mid-1970s. But since then, Japanese industry has operated predominantly to the right of the threshold, K, in figure 17. And the number of Japanese companies on the right of that threshold has increased steadily. Evidencing that corporate behavior is the uniquely manic investment trend that Japan demonstrates in figure 16. Analysts have advanced diverse reasons for Japan's economic sluggishness since the 1990s. What we need to recognize is that the fundamental reason for that sluggishness is Japanese companies' behavior.

Let's see what would happen if companies pursued optimal levels of capital intensiveness. To begin with, production output would mirror the availability of labor. Industry can always manufacture more equipment, but the amount of available labor is a fixed quantity. Maximizing value-added and economic growth thus becomes a matter of accepting the amount of production output that available labor can support. In figure 17, that means limiting production output to the level indicated by the threshold, K. It means not trying to push production beyond that level by overinvesting in automation.

CORPORATE MANAGEMENT IN A SHRINKING-POPULATION ECONOMY

Automation, clearly, is the wrong way to cope with the labor shortage that will occur in Japan as a result of population shrinkage and aging. The optimal level of production, meanwhile, depends on the amount of available labor. So corporate management in Japan's shrinking-population economy will be a matter of seeking to optimize corporate performance while accepting the inevitability of declining production. Corporate managers will need to learn from past mistakes and to avoid the temptation to automate their companies into oblivion.

Adopting the new mindset will be difficult. Continuously expanding production has long been an article of faith at Japanese companies. Maintaining production growth was why Japanese employers turned to middle-aged women when the 20-to-39-year-old labor pool began to shrink. Keeping production growing was also why they subsequently responded to the shrinkage in the labor pool with all-out automation.

The main reason for Japanese industry's obsession with expanding production has been technological weakness. Notwithstanding the vaunted international competitiveness of some Japanese manufacturers, most Japanese companies have lagged their North American and European competitors technologically. And they have sought to compensate for that disadvantage through economies of scale. So a decline in production volumes is a strategic threat to Japanese competitiveness.

An expanding population would offer the hope of renewed production growth after Japanese industry had redressed its present excess capacity. But Japan's shrinking workforce will oblige industry to follow that corrective reduction in production with further reductions. Failing to do so would have dire economic consequences. The author's economic forecast for Japan is an extension of economic theory. Underlying the forecast is the assumption that companies seek to optimize their capital intensiveness. If companies maintain a capital intensiveness that is other than optimal, Japan's economy will underperform the author's forecast.

The challenge for corporate management in Japan is threefold: optimize production volumes, produce efficiently, and pay wages and salaries that are appropriate. Companies have nothing to fear from Japan's shrinking-population economy as long as their managements address these challenges. Likewise, Japanese will continue to enjoy a high living standard if their companies behave responsibly. That's because a sound and effective response to the threefold challenge cited here will maximize national income.

Maximizing national income is all the more important in view of the impossibility of economic growth in a shrinking population. Japanese can ill afford to squander resources that are essential to maintaining a satisfactory standard of living. What Japan needs to aim for economically is the fulfillment of its potential growth rate—the rate that results from using labor and capital resources optimally. Japan's potential rate of economic growth will decline and ultimately turn negative as the workforce shrinks.

Toward a Consumption-Driven Economy

JAPAN'S INVESTMENT-DRIVEN ECONOMY

What most distinguishes Japan's economy from the U.S. and European economies is the far-higher rate of investment in Japan. Figure 18 shows the gross formation of fixed capital as a percentage of GDP in principal industrialized nations. We define gross fixed capital formation as the sum of private-sector capital spending, public works investment, and housing investment. In recent years, gross fixed capital formation in Japan has been about 30% of GDP, compared with only about 20% in the United States and western Europe.

Japan's high investment rate is easy to understand from the perspective of capital spending. That investment is for expanding production capacity, and expanded production increases the nation's GDP. Capital spending, in other words, is investment in increasing Japan's future income. The same is true of public works investment and housing investment. Readers might question the connection of public works and housing to production. But Japan's national accounts include monetary equivalents of the convenience and other benefits conferred by public works and housing. That is in accordance with the guidelines adopted by the United Nations in its System of National Accounts. So we also regard public

Figure 18
Gross Fixed Capital Formation as a Percentage of GDP in
Principal Industrialized Nations

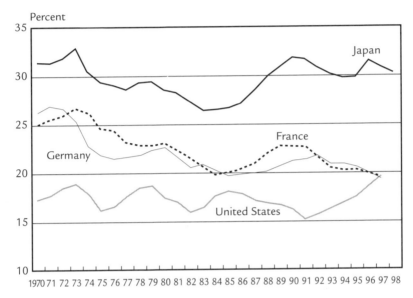

Source: Annual national accounts data published by the OECD

works investment and housing investment as means of increasing Japan's future income.

The other component of GDP is consumption. Whereas investment is for increasing future income, consumption is for maintaining and raising people's living standards now. Japan's comparatively high rate of investment means that Japanese have given higher priority to raising living standards in the future than today. Envisioning inversions of the curves in figure 18 gives a good picture of the rates of consumption in different nations.

People frequently cite traditional Japanese diligence as the reason for Japan's high investment rate. That explanation, however, collapses under careful scrutiny. Japan's average investment rate in the prewar span from 1930 to 1935 was only 11.6%. So ethnic disposition scarcely accounts for the disparity in investment rates seen in figure 18. Technological progress, to be sure, has occasioned an increase in the scale of investment. But that is far from sufficient to account for the magnitude of the increase in Japan's investment rate.

A more-convincing reason for Japan's high investment rate is a fundamental change in national policy that occurred immediately after World War II. The nation faced a critical shortage of food, clothing, and other goods essential to daily life. Policy makers debated two basic options for addressing that shortage: tackle the shortage directly by promoting the production of the daily essentials among consumer goods or tackle it indirectly by promoting the production of such capital goods as basic materials and manufacturing equipment. The government ultimately adopted the latter option, or the "detour production" espoused famously by University of Tokyo professor Arisawa Hiromi. And that decision shaped Japan's postwar economic development definitively.

The government's decision seems reasonable enough in retrospect. Inflation was raging, and the surging demand for consumer goods threatened to undermine Japan's supply capacity by diminishing savings. The question remains, though, as to why Japan needed to produce all of its capital goods domestically. Japan's balance of payments might have limited the scope for relying on imports. But Japan surely didn't need integrated, capital-intensive industries for producing a full range of basic goods, such as steel, ceramics, and chemicals. That's what happened, however, under the priority production system advanced vigorously by the government.

In 1952, the Japanese government established the Central Council for Savings Promotion, which continues to operate as the Central Council for Financial Services Information. That council called on the populace to restrain consumption and to deposit funds in savings accounts, and it encouraged banks forcefully to lend funds to companies in the designated priority sectors. This was the beginning of the so-called convoy system, where the government defined a common policy for the financial industry and dissuaded banks from deviating from that policy. The government accompanied that policy with the rationing of imported materials in accordance with its industrial priorities. All of this had the effect of stimulating huge investment in expanding the production of capital goods, and capital spending rose sharply as a percentage of GDP. Japan's unusually high investment rate dates from that stage in the postwar era.

MASSIVE CAPITAL GOODS INDUSTRIES

Having a high investment rate is enough in itself to qualify as an investment-led economy. But Japan reinforced its investment-led qualifications by deploying a full line of capital goods industries. Most of Japan's best-known corporations produce such capital goods as steel, ceramics, chemicals, heavy electrical equipment, heavy machinery, construction materials, and others.

The structure of demand shifted in the mid-1970s. Demand surged for small, high-value-added items, such as semiconductor devices, and demand for large capital goods languished. As we would expect, that shift occasioned a decline in Japan's investment rate. The rate turned upward again in the early 1980s, thanks to the manic investment in automation that we have examined and to a surge in public works spending. But although investment in automation increased demand for machinery industries, it did little for the basic materials industries or for the construction industry. Burgeoning public works spending was an effort to offset the declining private-sector demand for those industries. That spending drove Japan's public sector to the brink of fiscal collapse, however, and contributed to the nation's prolonged economic stagnation.

Japan's high investment rate and its preponderance of massive capital goods industries are clearly attributable to consistent government policy. In turn, they have forced policy makers to continue to concentrate on investment. Government attention has riveted on trends in capital spending, and consumer spending has been a secondary consideration. This has earned ridicule from American and European observers, who have characterized Japan's policy makers as the "last true Keynesians."

Economic policy in Japan has reflected a general pattern of thinking that favors future income over present consumption. In contrast, people in the West, especially in the United States, have devoted higher priority to living and spending for today. That pattern of thought, had it prevailed in Japan, would have precluded the development of an investment-led economy. Market forces and government policy would have steered the Japanese economy in a very different direction.

Now, Japanese will need to rethink their economic perspective. The economic ramifications of population shrinkage will be every bit as profound as Japan's postwar economic realignment. They will force Japanese

Figure 19

Gross Investment as a Percentage of GDP in Comparison with Consumption and Gross Investment

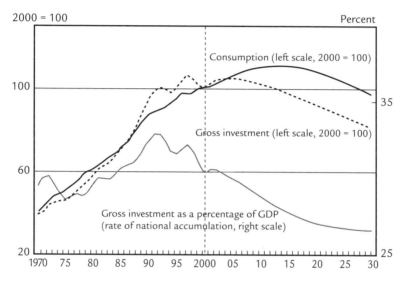

Sources: Annual national accounts data for the years to 2000 and projections by the author for subsequent years

to choose between highly contrasting economic frameworks. We will examine the choices that will confront Japanese in chapter 6.

DECLINING INVESTMENT AS A RESULT OF DEMOGRAPHIC AGING

Figure 10 (page 32) shows how a shrinking workforce will make a lasting decline in capital spending inevitable. Investment, however, includes public works investment and housing investment, as well as capital spending. Mathematically, it also includes net exports. A surplus of exports over imports means a reduction in national expenditures. It means that Japanese are essentially lending resources to foreigners temporarily. Net exports are equivalent to foreign investment, since a surplus in the current account requires a matching deficit in the capital account.

We have examined domestic investment as gross fixed capital formation, and we need to consider each component of that investment in preparing projections for Japan's investment rate. Daunting unknowns, however, obscure the outlook for public works investment, which is subject to changing government attitudes, and for foreign investment, which is subject to economic trends in importing nations. So we will approach our subject from the standpoint of the national savings rate.

The national savings rate is equivalent to the investment rate, as we saw in our discussion on pages 60 to 64. That is, the mechanism of the savings-investment balance ensures that the sum of personal savings, corporate savings, and government savings remains equal to the sum of capital spending, public works investment, and housing investment.

Figure 19 presents a forecast for Japan's national savings rate based on a mathematical function developed by the author. The gross investment rate and, identically, the national savings rate appear as the thin solid line. Demographic aging means a decline in the economically active percentage of the population and a decline in overall capacity for savings. This trend is already evident in actual economic results. Japan's savings rate has been trending downward since the early 1990s, and the aging of the population is a big reason for that trend. In other words, demographic aging is depressing the investment rate, and it will affect Japan's investment-led economic framework greatly.

MOVING TO A CONSUMPTION-LED ECONOMY

The author has prepared projections for gross investment and for consumption on the basis of the forecast for the national savings rate. Those projections indicate that gross investment will slip below the 2000 level in 2013 and that, in 2030, it will be 19.4% lower than in 2000. Consumption, on the other hand, continues growing in the author's projections until 2013. It peaks at a level 10.8% higher than the 2000 level, and even after an extended decline, it is only 3.2% lower than that 2000 level in 2030.

Consumption will thus replace investment as the driving dynamic of the Japanese economy. That transition is unavoidable, irrespective of government policy or corporate behavior. The decline in the savings rate caused by the aging of the population will impose an ineluctable limit on investment. Any effort to undertake investment in excess of that limit would encounter a lack of resources. Japanese could import resources to raise their investment rate temporarily above the level indicated in figure 19, but that would entail accepting a deficit in the nation's international balance of payments. The United States has been able to run perennial balance-of-payments deficits because the dollar is the main currency for international transactions. But Japan could not remain in deficit for long, and its investment rate could not remain above the level indicated in figure 19 for an extended period.

Japan's investment rate will remain high by international standards even as the nation shifts to a consumption-led economy. The Japanese investment rate will be 26.6% as late as 2030, which is substantially higher than the present U.S. and European rates. Japan thus will still have an economic framework that favors future income over present consumption. But the decline in the investment rate could occasion a change in Japanese economic thinking.

Figure 19 traces economic changes that will result from the aging of society, but the author has predicated the calculations on the economic thinking that prevails in Japan today. Changing attitudes could cause investment to be lower and consumption higher than the projections in figure 19. However, that would amplify the impending decline in production capacity and reduce Japan's economy to a size smaller than the author has projected. That economic shrinkage would be a reflection of the will of the Japanese people and should therefore not be subject to reproach. But this is a controversial issue, so the author has elected to predicate his projections on present-day economic attitudes.

A CHANGING CORPORATE LANDSCAPE

The projections in figure 19 hold tremendous significance for Japanese corporations. They denote structural change in Japanese industry: rapid decline for capital goods industries and growth for consumer goods industries and service industries. Even the growth in consumer goods and services, however, will be subject to the general downturn in economic scale. Managements in those sectors will need to be just as attentive as their counterparts in the capital goods sector to the new realities. Companies in every sector will need to tailor their capital spending programs carefully and realistically to trends in demand and labor. Also complicating management in the consumer goods and service sectors will be the growing diversity of demand, which we will examine later. That will occasion a large disparity in sales performance among companies in those sectors.

Another facet of the structural change in Japanese industry will be change in the corporate hierarchy. Japan's capital goods industries rely on numerous peripheral industries, and each of them therefore supports a vast penumbra of industries and companies. The huge value-added generated by those industrial groupings is essential to Japan's consumer goods industries and service industries. Capital goods industries thus occupy the summit of Japan's corporate hierarchy. That hierarchy has changed somewhat in recent years, but in matters of economic policy the voice of Japanese business still speaks most loudly of capital goods. And companies' and industries' interests reflect their position in the vertical relationships of their industrial pyramids.

The rise of consumer goods industries and service industries, along with the growing diversity of demand, will reduce the importance of vertical, pyramidal relationships. Those industries are less integrally dependent on peripheral industries than are their counterparts in the capital goods sector. Companies will therefore adopt more-independent stances in their dealings with each other. Conflicts of interest will become more common. That will weaken a traditional feature of Japanese management: generally harmonious coordination in and among industrial sectors. It will dilute the ties between companies in the same corporate groups and between companies and their suppliers and their suppliers' suppliers. Japan's marketplace will be the scene of increasingly fierce competition. Managements accustomed to comparative peace and harmony will need to learn to cope with a more-aggressive mode of industrial behavior.

THE GROWING DIFFICULTY OF DIVERSIFICATION

We will conclude this chapter with a comment on diversification as a corporate strategy. Companies typically enter new lines of business when they encounter or perceive limits to sales and earnings growth in their traditional business. Diversification spurred by that motivation will become increasingly common as the composition of Japanese demand changes. However, the prospects for successful diversification will dwindle in Japan's shrinking-population economy.

Companies in Japan have rarely faced a truly precipitous decline in demand in their traditional, core operations. Overall demand has continued to grow, and diversification has been a viable means of compensating for gradually declining earnings or even modest losses in traditional lines of business. Everything will change, however, in the shrinking-population economy. Companies might survive by shifting completely to new lines of business. But simply dabbling in new ventures while persevering in traditional businesses that have become unviable will prove disastrous. Companies will need to move swiftly to pare or even close down unprofitable operations that offer little prospect of recovery. Maintaining idle or underutilized assets will be suicidal.

Allocating assets forthrightly to viable operations will be good for the Japanese economy overall, as well as for individual companies. We saw in figure 14 (page 50) that Japan's continuing decline in marginal productivity has been unusual among the industrialized nations. Japanese productivity has suffered especially since the 1990s from companies clinging to core operations that are no longer viable. Marginal productivity in North America and Europe is level or rising. That is partly because of technological progress. But it is also because companies shed inefficient production capacity ruthlessly during the recessionary years of the 1980s. Japan's shrinking-population economy will present a stark choice for companies that become unable to generate viable value-added in traditional operations: close down or move into new lines of business.

CHAPTER III

Sharing the Wealth: Reducing Regional Disparity in Economic Vitality

PRESSURE ON THE METROPOLISES

A METROPOLITAN LEAD IN AGING

Concern about the shrinking and aging of Japan's population appears to be stronger outside the nation's largest metropolises. Depopulation is already a serious problem in several nonmetropolitan parts of Japan, and people in those parts of the nation rue the potential socioeconomic effects of a further decline in population. They note that the continuing influx of largely young people into Japan's largest metropolises will offset the effects of population shrinkage and aging in those cities. They are right about population shrinkage proceeding faster in nonmetropolitan Japan than in big Japanese cities, but they are wrong about aging. Aging will proceed faster in the big cities than elsewhere.

Population shrinkage will be slower in Japan's large cities than elsewhere in the nation because the metropolitan populations have larger percentages of young people and smaller percentages of old people. For example, the over-65 percentage of the population in Greater Tokyo— Tokyo and its neighboring prefectures of Kanagawa, Chiba, and Saitama— was 14.4% in 2000, but it was fully 24.8% in Shimane Prefecture, home to the fastest-aging population in all of Japan's 47 prefectures. Most of the over-65 Japanese will die over the next decade or two, which ensures a higher rate of population shrinkage outside Japan's metropolises.

In contrast, the higher percentage of young people in the metropolises ensures a higher pace of aging. The segments of today's population most likely to survive as over-65 residents in 2030 are men aged 35 to 48 and women aged 35 to 53. Those segments accounted for 24.1% of Greater Tokyo's population in 2000. That was nearly 10 percentage points higher than the over-65 percentage of the population. So the over-65 percentage of the population in Greater Tokyo is bound to rise. Tokyoites older than 65 numbered a little more than 4.8 million in 2000, and that number will approximately double, to between 8.6 million and 8.9 million in 2030.

Shimane Prefecture, on the other hand, will host a decline in the over-65 percentage of the population. As of 2000, Shimane residents likely to survive as over-65 residents in 2030 accounted for 22.4% of the population. That was lower than the over-65 percentage of the population—24.8%—in 2000. To be sure, nonmetropolitan prefectures receive a net influx of middle-aged people who return home after spending their careers in Japan's metropolises. But even accounting for that influx, the over-65 residents of Shimane will likely number 180,000 to 200,000 in 2030. That would mean little change from Shimane's population of 189,000 over-65 residents in 2000.

The lesson of these projections is the rapid aging in store for Japan's largest cities. Accompanying the comparatively slow population decline in those metropolises will be sharp growth in the over-65 percentage of the population.

DEMOGRAPHIC CONTRASTS: TOKYO AND SHIMANE

In mapping Japanese demographic trends geographically, we need to account for the movement of people between prefectures. The assumptions that we make about that movement will affect our population projections greatly. Japan's government conducts a national census every five years, and demographic researchers in Japan therefore tend to deal with geographical population shifts in five-year increments. We ordinarily base our assumptions about future movements of people on the movements recorded in the past five years. That is the methodology employed by Japan's National Institute of Population and Social Security Research in preparing population estimates for different prefectures.

Figure 20
Population Composition by Age in Greater Tokyo
and in Shimane Prefecture

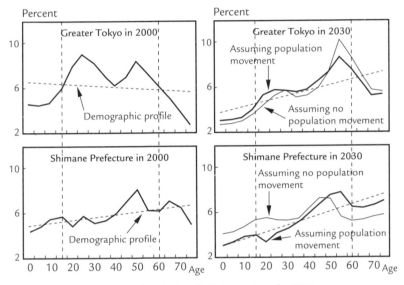

Sources: Census data for 2000 and projections by Fujimasa Iwao for 2030

Five-year movements in population are of dubious value, however, as a basis for long-term population projections of 30 years or so. For example, the population movements between the censuses of 1995 and 2000 took place amid prolonged economic stagnation. That stagnation drove increased numbers of people to large cities in search of work. Meanwhile, it also increased the number of middle-aged and older people who lost their jobs in the city through restructuring and who as a result returned home to outlying regions.

The author here accompanies projections that include an assumed pattern of population movement with projections that assume no movement. These projections thus account for maximal and minimal effects on regional demographics from population movement. These differing assumptions are the reason for the possible demographic ranges projected above and below for Greater Tokyo and Shimane Prefecture in 2030.

Figure 20 presents a comparison of population composition by age in Greater Tokyo and in Shimane Prefecture in 2000 and in 2030. Distinguishing Tokyo's demographic profile in 2000 is a heavy concentration in the 20s and 30s age groups—the large peak on the left side of the graph. That peak is a lot higher than the corresponding peak in figure 2 (page 25), which presents the demographic profile for Japan overall. Tokyo's population thus has a youthful weighting, especially in comparison with Shimane Prefecture's population, also profiled in figure 20.

The graphs in figure 20 include trend lines for the composition of population by age. The straight dotted lines follow paths that equalize the aggregate areas above and below the trend lines and inside the curves. The angles of these population structure lines furnish interesting comparative insights into demographics. They allow for comparing different populations across the entire age spectrum. The more sharply a line angles upward to the right, the higher is the age weighting in the population overall. That supports more-revealing comparisons than we get from simply comparing the over-65 percentage of the populations.

In figure 20, the population structure lines for Greater Tokyo and Shimane Prefecture in 2000 move in opposite directions. Both lines angle upward to the right, however, in the graphs for 2030, and their upward angles are almost identical. The population structure lines for 2030 in figure 20 are for the population structure as adjusted for the movement of people. So Tokyo and Shimane will have similar demographics in 2030 even in the unlikely event that recent trends in population movement continue.

A LOT FEWER JAPANESE IN THEIR 20S AND 30S

The recent influx of population into Greater Tokyo has centered on young age brackets. We might wonder, then, why the Tokyo and Shimane demographics should converge in 2030. The chief reason is an impending nationwide decline in the number of young people.

Japan's population, as we have seen, will shrink 14.0% by 2030, compared with 2000. The shrinkage will be fully 32.9%, however, in the population aged 20 to 39. Even if people in that age range continue moving to Greater Tokyo at the recent rate, their number will decline, and their share of the overall population will decline, too.

People aged 20 to 39 numbered more than 10.6 million in Greater Tokyo in 2000. That number is poised to decline 33.3%, to 7.1 million, in 2030, even assuming a continuing influx of people. Meanwhile, the number of over-65 Tokyoites, as we have seen, is likely to increase 84.6%, to 8.9 million in 2030, from a little more than 4.8 million in 2000.

Shimane Prefecture's inhabitants in their 20s and 30s numbered 160,000 in 2000. Their number is poised to decline 35.6%, to just over 100,000, in 2030. That decline is slightly more rapid than the national average, and it reflects the expected movement of people out of the prefecture. However, the number of over-65 residents of Shimane will increase only 6.5%, likely rising, as we have seen, to just over 200,000 in 2030, from just under 190,000 in 2000. The right-trending angle of Shimane's population structure line will continue to move upward somewhat, but the increase will be far smaller than the change in Tokyo's line, and the angles will thus converge.

We need to note another important factor in Greater Tokyo demographics: a birthrate that is lower than the national average. That will cause Greater Tokyo's 20-to-39 population to shrink faster than the national average despite an inflow of people, and it will spur the rapid aging of the region's demographic profile.

As of 1995, the birthrate in the four prefectures that we define as Greater Tokyo ranged from 1.13 in Tokyo proper to 1.41 in Saitama Prefecture. The overall birthrate in Greater Tokyo was thus lower than the national average of 1.44 and far lower than Shimane Prefecture's birthrate of 1.75. That is why the under-30 percentage of the population appears lower for Tokyo than for Shimane in the graph lines for stationary population (figure 20). Tokyo's population structure line would move upward to the right even more sharply if we excluded inflows of population.

Greater Tokyo, incidentally, was home to some 30.8% of Japan's population in the 20-to-39 age bracket in 2000. In our projections for 2030, that figure will decline slightly, to 30.5%, including geographical population shifts. Inflows of population will be insufficient to fully offset the declining number of births in Greater Tokyo.

DEMOGRAPHIC AGING OF UNMANAGEABLE SPEED IN JAPAN'S METROPOLISES

We have seen that the human movement toward Japan's metropolises will hardly forestall the adverse effects of demographic aging and shrinkage there. We have also seen (in chapter 1) that the most daunting economic effects of Japan's aging will result from the unmanageably rapid pace of that phenomenon. That rapidity is a bigger problem than however high the over-65 percentage of the population might become. We have seen, too, that the implications of aging will weigh most heavily on Tokyo and on Japan's other metropolises.

Of special note is the difference in the speed of aging between Japan's metropolitan and nonmetropolitan areas. The over-65 percentage of Greater Tokyo's population is poised to rise to 28.2% in 2030, including geographical shifts, and to 30.1%, excluding those shifts, from 14.4% in 2000. In Shimane Prefecture, the likely increase will be to 33.7%, including geographical shifts, and to 27.8%, excluding those shifts, from 24.8%.

The issue of declining family size will become especially acute in Japan's metropolises, especially Tokyo, as young people converge on those areas. That issue will be of little importance in Japan's nonmetropolitan areas, which are on the other side of the nation's population shifts. An absolute decline in population will proceed more rapidly in Shimane Prefecture, however, than in Greater Tokyo and in other Japanese metropolitan areas. Shimane's population is likely to decline 21.8% from its 2000 level by 2030, including geographical shifts, and 15.7%, excluding those shifts. Tokyo's likely population decline will be only 5.5%, including geographical shifts, and 14.8%, excluding those shifts.

Interestingly, economic shrinkage will be smaller in Shimane Prefecture than in Greater Tokyo. The economic growth rate closely reflects trends in the size of the working-age population. Consequently, Japan's metropolises face bigger issues than the nation's nonmetropolitan areas do in regard to economic growth rate and per capita income. We will now examine more precisely the factors in regional economic disparities.

A BIG DECLINE IN STORE FOR THE WORKING-AGE POPULATION IN JAPAN'S METROPOLISES

Figure 21 shows the expected changes between 2000 and 2030 in the total population and in the working-age population in Japan's prefectures. For the 2030 figures, the author has used the average of the projections inclusive and exclusive of population movement. That is partly an effort to simplify the graph. It is also in recognition of the extremes of population

Figure 21

Rate of Decline in Overall Population and in Working-Age Population
from 2000 to 2030

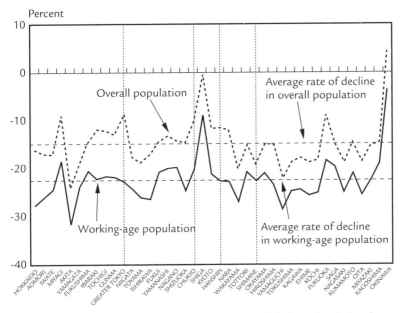

Percent

Overall population

Average rate of decline
in overall population

Working-age population

Average rate of decline
in working-age population

Sources: Census data for 2000 and an average of projections inclusive and exclusive of
population movement for 2030

movement and stability that those projections represent.

Overall population decline is smallest by far in the three main metropolitan areas of Greater Tokyo; Hanshin (Osaka and Hyogo prefectures); and Chukyo (Aichi, Gifu, and Mie prefectures) and in the two
regional urban areas of Miyagi Prefecture and Fukuoka Prefecture. The
horizontal lines for average decline in overall population and in working-age population represent simple averages of the prefectural totals,
not national percentage declines. Overall population shrinkage exceeds
the average in nearly all of the nonmetropolitan prefectures.

Two exceptions to the trend in nonmetropolitan prefectures in figure
21 are Shiga, where the decline in population is insignificant, and Okinawa,
where the population is growing. The apparently insignificant decline in
population in Shiga is a statistical anomaly. Shiga has been the scene of
a factory building boom in recent years. That has occasioned an influx
of population during the period that is the basis for the statistical

projections in figure 21, and it has thus inflated the statistical component that includes geographical population movement. Okinawa, meanwhile, differs notably from its "mainland" counterparts in climate and lifestyle. The archipelago prefecture has an extremely high birthrate, at 1.87, and an especially long average life expectancy.

Note that the disparity between overall and working-age population trends is more pronounced in Greater Tokyo, Hanshin, and Chukyo and in some other prefectures than in most of Japan's prefectures. The three large metropolitan areas show smaller-than-average declines in overall population but basically match the average for the decline in working-age population.

Greater Tokyo's projected decline in working-age population is actually larger than the average. And some prefectures that show larger-than-average declines in overall population, especially in western Japan, show smaller-than-average declines in working-age population. These differentials reflect differing paces of aging. Aging will proceed faster than the average in the large metropolitan areas, and that will cause larger-than-average declines in working-age population.

ABSOLUTE AND RELATIVE DECLINES IN ECONOMIC GROWTH IN JAPAN'S METROPOLISES

Changes in relative standing in economic growth rates are implicit in the expected rates of decline in working-age population. That principle applies domestically just as it applies internationally. In Japan, the working-age population is poised to decline most precipitously in Akita Prefecture, followed by the prefectures of Yamaguchi, Hokkaido, Wakayama, Ishikawa, Toyama, and Aomori. Those prefectures are therefore likely to suffer the largest percentage declines in economic growth.

Of Japan's three main metropolises, Greater Tokyo has the 23rd-smallest expected decline in working-age population among the 41 regions (38 prefectures and 3 multiple-prefecture metropolitan areas) cited in figure 21; Hanshin the 19th smallest; and Chukyo the 9th smallest. This suggests a profound departure from the pattern in which economic growth rates have been highest in and around Japan's largest metropolises.

The Japanese regions that had the highest economic growth rates from 1975 to 1998 (the latter year being the most recent for which consistent comparative data is available) were Shiga, Nara, Ibaraki, Gunma,

Tochigi, and Yamanashi prefectures, followed by Chukyo and Greater Tokyo. The prefectures named are all adjacent to the three largest metropolitan regions. They predominate among the Japanese regions that had the highest percentage growth in working-age population during the same time span: Shiga, Nara, Okinawa, Ibaraki, Greater Tokyo, Miyagi, Chukyo, Tochigi, Fukuoka, Gunma, Shizuoka, and Yamanashi.

Greater Tokyo and Shimane Prefecture, at opposite ends of the aging spectrum, were our choice earlier for demographic comparisons. Let us return to those two regions and see how they fared economically between 1975 and 1998. Real income increased 2.1-fold during that span in Greater Tokyo and 1.8-fold in Shimane Prefecture. Working-age population, however, declined 8.8% in Shimane while increasing 28.5% in Tokyo.

So we need nuance our interpretation of the linkage between economic growth and working-age population growth. The two regions are likely to have similar percentage declines in working-age population between 2000 and 2030: 22.7% in Tokyo and 22.6% in Shimane. We will employ a model to examine the economic implications of the two regions' demographic prospects. What we will find is that aging is a more-influential factor than population shrinkage in economic performance.

THE AGING-CAUSED DECLINE IN LABOR PRODUCTIVITY

Another important factor for regional economic performance in Japan's shrinking and aging population will be the rising average age of the working-age population. Younger people, quite simply, produce more per hour than older people do. They are, in general, stronger, faster, and more adept with their hands. Envision two identical assembly lines, one staffed with young workers and the other staffed with old workers. We can be all but certain that the conveyor belt on the young workers' line will move faster than its counterpart staffed by old workers. So the aging of the workforce will affect labor productivity profoundly. And regional differences in the pace of aging will change prefectures' relative standing in productivity.

Mechanization can raise labor productivity, but it simply amplifies the productivity gap between young and old. Younger workers tend to be faster than their older counterparts in mastering new equipment. Young labor has been instrumental, for instance, in supporting the computerization of production processes in recent years.

The appeal of young labor for employers thus stems in large part from the higher productivity of younger workers. That is in addition to the generally lower wages that prevail among younger workers. To be sure, older workers offer some advantages in regard to such criteria as management skills and overall judgment. But those capabilities are essential to only a small portion of the work performed in manufacturing industries. A younger weighting in personnel results in higher productivity in most phases of manufacturing work.

Economists regard labor productivity as a reflection of capital intensiveness and of the quality of the workforce. Two important determinants of the quality of labor are educational levels and health standards. But these factors ordinarily receive attention only in discussions of differentials between industrialized nations and developing nations. The quality of labor has rarely arisen as an issue in discussions of labor productivity confined to industrialized nations. Those discussions have tended to center on capital intensiveness and on industrial structure. Aging in industrialized nations, however, makes the quality of labor a pressing issue. Aging depresses the average quality of the workforce and lowers labor productivity.

TURNING POINTS AT THE AGES OF 20 AND 55

All of this begs the question: At what age does the quality of labor begin to deteriorate? On an individual basis, the answer varies widely by industry, by job description, and by personal circumstances. A cross-sectional analysis of the workforce overall, however, reveals age-related turning points in labor productivity.

Our cross section consists of data for labor productivity and for the age structure of the workforce in each region of Japan. We will determine the age range in which a preponderance of labor results in a marked increase in labor productivity. Determining upper and lower thresholds accounts for the effects of knowledge and experience on the quality of labor. Our analysis reveals that the quality of labor declines markedly below the age of 20 and above the age of 55.

Figure 22 compares labor productivity with the percentage of the workforce aged 20 to 54 for each prefecture or metropolitan region of

Japan. We see a strong correlation between the relative youth of the work-force and labor productivity. The basis for figure 22 is data from 1995. But data from 1980 reveals the same basic pattern. That is, the correlation between age and labor productivity is most pronounced when we use the ages of 20 and 55 for the lower and upper thresholds.

We have several reasons to focus on the years 1980 and 1995. National censuses are our only reliable source of data for the age of the workforce by region, and Japan conducts a census every five years. Economic data, meanwhile, is only available in a consistent, regionally comparative for-mat up to 1998, as noted elsewhere. Another reason for focusing on 1980 and 1995 is that Japan's economy underwent structural change after the oil crises of the 1970s. In addition, the intervening census years of 1985 and 1990 were subject to the distortions of Japan's bubble economy.

THE AGE STRUCTURE OF THE WORKFORCE AND THE STRUCTURE OF INDUSTRY

Figure 22 leaves us to wonder about the cause-and-effect relationship between the relative youth of the workforce and labor productivity in different regions. Labor productivity is highest in manufacturing, espe-cially in large-scale manufacturing. The high productivity in large-scale manufacturing is principally the result of advanced mechanization; that is, of high capital intensiveness. And manufacturers seek younger work-ers to operate highly mechanized production systems efficiently. This trend leads several analysts to conclude that a young weighting in the work-force is the result, rather than the cause, of high labor productivity.

We can equally well conclude, however, that high-productivity indus-tries congregate in regions that offer relatively young workforces. That would explain the concentration of high-productivity, large-scale manu-facturing in Japan's three main metropolitan areas and in their surrounding prefectures. A less-young weighting in the workforce in those regions would presumably result in a lower concentration of large-scale manu-facturing. Conversely, we would presumably see a higher concentration of industries that can make do with older workers. Industries arise in the presence of demand and labor. Japan's vast diversity of industries—notwithstanding their widely varying levels of labor productivity—evi-dences that truism.

The percentage of Japan's population aged 20 to 54 that resided in

Figure 22

The Age Composition of the Workforce and Labor Productivity (1995)

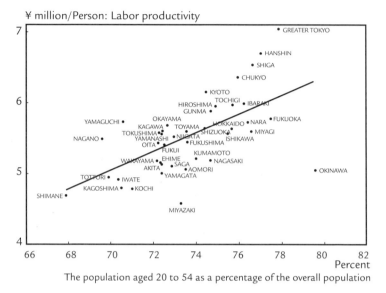

¥ million/Person: Labor productivity

The population aged 20 to 54 as a percentage of the overall population

Sources: Census data and prefectural economic data published by the Economic
Planning Agency (now part of the Cabinet Office)

the nation's three main metropolises surged to 55.0% in 1975, from
45.7% in 1950. That surge resulted partly from the rising percentage of
Japanese who continued on to university after high school. Japan's metropolises are home to an overwhelming majority of the nation's universities,
and the biggest population shift occurred among university-aged Japanese.
The high concentration of universities in Japan's metropolitan areas thus
appears to have fortified the foundation for high labor productivity.

Whatever the reasons for the relative youthfulness of Japan's metropolises, it will affect the geographic distribution of economic vitality profoundly. The very youthfulness of metropolitan Japan means that aging
will proceed faster in the big cities than elsewhere. And that will happen
even if people continue to move to the cities. An aging population means
an aging workforce, which means declining labor productivity. Economic
shrinkage in Japan's metropolises will thus proceed even faster than we
might infer from the decrease in working-age population.

A RAPIDLY AGING URBAN WORKFORCE

Let's take a look at likely trends in the age composition of labor by region. We'll use the same method that we used to project structural trends in the age composition of Japanese labor overall. That is, we'll assume a continuation of the trends that have prevailed since 1975 in the percentage of working women and of working elderly. Figure 23 shows our findings for the percentages of the workforce aged 20 to 54 in each prefecture and region in 1995 and in 2030. Except for the bar for Shimane Prefecture, the top of each bar in the graph indicates the percentage in 1995, and the bottom of each bar indicates the projected percentage in 2030. Shimane is the only prefecture or region where the projected percentage in 2030 is higher than the 1995 percentage, and its bar expresses that inverted range.

The biggest projected decline in the 20-to-54 percentage of the workforce is in Tokyo. In 1995, the 20-to-54 percentage the workforce was higher in Tokyo, at 77.9%, than in any other prefecture or region except Okinawa. That percentage is poised to plunge to 65.2% in 2030, the lowest level among the 41 prefectures and regions cited. The next-largest projected declines in the 20-to-54 percentage of the workforce are mainly in Japan's other large metropolises and in their surrounding prefectures: Hanshin, Ibaraki, Ishikawa, Chukyo, Kyoto, Tochigi, Shizuoka, Nara, Gunma, and Hiroshima.

After Tokyo, Nagano Prefecture has the lowest projected figure for the 20-to-54 percentage of the workforce in 2030, followed by Yamanashi, Kyoto, Shizuoka, Ishikawa, Gunma, Yamaguchi, Chukyo, Ibaraki, and Tochigi. Of greater concern than the 20-to-54 percentage in 2030, however, is the decline in that percentage. That is because of the changes in industrial structure and in labor productivity that will result from an aging workforce. And as noted above, that aging will occur most rapidly in Tokyo and in Japan's other large metropolitan areas.

Nagano and Yamaguchi prefectures, for instance, show two of the lowest figures for the 20-to-54 percentage of the workforce in 2030. But the decline in that percentage is smaller in those two prefectures than in most other prefectures. So the changes in industrial structure and the declines in labor productivity will also be relatively small in those two prefectures, and the economic effects of aging will be minimal. Note in figure 22 that labor productivity in Nagano and Yamaguchi prefectures

Figure 23

Change in the Age 20-to-54 Percentage of the Workforce
from 1995 to 2030 (declines for every prefecture and region except
Shimane, where the change is positive)

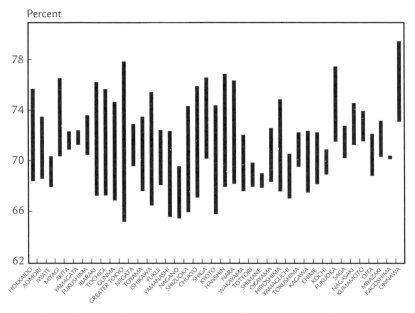

Sources: Census data for 1995 and an average of projections inclusive and exclusive of
population movement for 2030

is high for their age demographics. Although they will have two of Japan's
oldest workforces in 2030, that doesn't mean that they will rank near the
bottom in labor productivity.

Also note in figure 22 that Japan's three largest metropolises and their
neighboring prefectures are at the extreme upper right of the graph. Their
high labor productivity, in other words, has a strong correlation with
their exceedingly young workforces. Rapid aging in the metropolises will
produce stunning changes in industrial structure and precipitous declines
in labor productivity. In terms of figure 22, the metropolises and their
prefectural neighbors will slip toward the lower left of the graph.

We saw in chapter 2 that Japan's national income is likely to decline
about 15% between 2000 and 2030. Economic decline will be even sharper, however, in regions where the workforces shrink and age more than the
national average. Similarly, average per capita income will decline in the

regions of Japan where the working-age percentage of the population declines. Per capita income in Japan is likely to change little between 2000 and 2030, as we will see in chapter 5, but it will decline sharply in the nation's metropolises. And that will mean a decline in living standards there.

So Japan urgently needs to begin preparing to cope with the regional economic effects of population shrinkage and aging. And the need for well-conceived preparation is most pressing in the nation's metropolitan areas.

The Impending Redistribution of Economic Vitality

APPROACHES TO REGIONAL ECONOMIC FORECASTING

Macroeconomic models are the standard tools for economic forecasting, and the author employed a macroeconomic model to prepare the economic forecast for Japan discussed in chapter 2. Macroeconomic models therefore would seem a natural choice for preparing economic forecasts for Japan's regions. Alas, macroeconomic models have critical limitations as tools for regional economic forecasting. That is because of the heavy weighting of interregional commerce in the economies of Japan's prefectures.

Gross demand in Shimane Prefecture, for example, was about ¥2.5 trillion in 2000. The prefecture's purchasing from other regions to help meet that demand totaled about ¥1.6 trillion, and its sales to other regions totaled about ¥1.4 trillion. Inflows of commodities thus fulfilled 63.1% of Shimane's gross demand in 2000, and outflows were equivalent to 55.6% of internal demand. In all 47 Japanese prefectures, inflows of commodities fulfilled an average of 60.5% of gross demand, and outflows were equivalent to 68.6% of internal demand.

Economic modeling for any prefecture thus needs to include assumptions about the volumes of commodity inflows and outflows. That means making implicit assumptions about trends in consumer spending and in capital spending in other regions. And these assumptions cover some two-thirds of the prefecture's economy. So the modeler has largely completed the economic forecast for the prefecture before even putting the model to work. In addition, the huge weighting of the initial assumptions in the forecast amplifies the distortion from the modeler's subjectivity.

Another problem with modeling in regional economic forecasting is the lack of enforced correlation with forecasts for the Japanese economy overall. The sum of the separate forecasts could easily differ greatly from the likely size of the national economy. Whether too high or too low, inaccurate regional forecasts undermine economic planning. Yet devising a model that addresses each prefecture objectively and appropriately while maintaining consistency with the national economy is fiendishly difficult. The author is aware of only a single full-scale model ever devised for that task. That was a model built by Japan's Economic Planning Agency (now part of the Cabinet Office) in 1969. The model was massive, but it doesn't seem to have been especially successful.

Economic interchange with other regions is also an important component of the Japanese economy overall. The forecast for Japan discussed in chapter 2 includes the assumption that trends in external economic relations will continue basically unchanged. But trade accounts for a far smaller portion of the national economy than interregional commerce accounts for in Japan's prefectural economies. Exports accounted for only 10.8% of the Japanese economy in 2000, and imports were equivalent to only 9.3%. So reasonable assumptions about trade are unlikely to distort model-based forecasts for the national economy greatly.

REGIONAL ECONOMIC FORECASTS BASED ON POPULATION

The author has elected to reconcile regional and national economic forecasting by approaching regional incomes as a distribution of national income. To the author's knowledge, this is the first formal application of that approach to forecasting regional trends by prefecture. We want to determine the regional economic effects of population shrinkage and aging, so our criteria for determining the regional distribution of national income need to address demographic factors. Our model, that is, should reveal the economic effects of demographic changes when other factors are constant. Conversely, our forecasts will not account for factors other than demographics that might affect economic trends differently in different prefectures. The Japanese government, for example, could move some central-government functions away from Tokyo, or Tokyo's financial center could move to another city. But those kinds of changes are for another model to address.

We have seen the strong correlation in each region between labor productivity and the age structure of the workforce. Our model will incorporate that correlation as a criterion for the distribution of national income. Full-time workers are more productive, however, than part-time workers, so our model will also account for changes in the full-time percentage of the workforce. That percentage is subject, though, to dauntingly complex influences, such as lifestyles and social infrastructure. So the author has opted for an admittedly rough indicator: gender. Males account for a disproportionately large percentage of full-time workers in Japan and females for a disproportionately large percentage of part-time workers. So we will refer to gender as an indicator of the full-time percentage of the workforce.

Another important variable in labor productivity is industrial density. Regions that have a high concentration of companies and industrial activity tend to enjoy logistical efficiencies in the movement of raw materials and semifinished goods. They also tend to enjoy high concentrations of useful information. Those and other advantages support generally higher levels of labor productivity. Japan's three largest metropolitan areas offer compelling examples of the higher labor productivity that results from those advantages. And population density is a good indicator of industrial density. An abundance of labor supports high concentrations of industry.

This completes our array of criteria for calculating income distribution on the basis of demographics. The next question is how accurately our population-based model will account for the geographical distribution of national income. We can learn a lot about the credibility of our model by applying it to historical data. Applying it as a cross-sectional model to the data for 1980 and for 1995 yields convincing multiple correlation coefficients of more than 0.8.

Imposing a single model on all of Japan's prefectures, however, invites unnecessary distortion. The author has therefore developed two versions of the model and has divided the nation's prefectures into two groups for economic modeling. Trial and error have refined the groupings, which reflect the commonalities of industrial structure, geographic economic affiliation, structure of employment, and cultural affinity. Interestingly, cross-checking the models against historical data has verified the existence of two distinct blocks in the Japanese economy. Standardization methodology, meanwhile, has ensured statistical consistency between the two models.

THE FORECASTS: (1) ASSUMING POPULATION MOVEMENT

Figures 24 and 25 show the percentage change in economic size that our models indicate for each prefecture and region from 1998 to 2030. As noted elsewhere, 1998 is the most recent year for which historically consistent economic data was available by prefecture. Figure 24 presents forecasts predicated on the assumption that population movement among prefectures will continue at the present rate. In figure 25, the assumption is that no population movement will occur.

Also shown in figures 24 and 25 are the projected increases in labor productivity and the projected declines in the workforce. Prefectural or regional income is the product of annual output per worker, net of capital depreciation, times the number of workers. And the graphs show the economic effects of the shrinkage and aging of the workforce in each prefecture and region.

We have seen that the aging of a workforce depresses labor productivity, but automation and other technological advances could more than offset that effect over the 32-year span covered in figures 24 and 25. Conversely, the aging of Japan's workforce will diminish the economic contribution we would otherwise expect from technological advances. We need to bear this in mind as a definitive feature of the shrinking-population economy.

Excepting only Shiga Prefecture and Okinawa Prefecture, every region in figure 24, which accounts for population movement, shows economic shrinkage. Twenty of the 41 prefectures and regions show economic shrinkage greater than the national average of 14.2%—the dotted line in the graphs. And as described elsewhere, a recent and presumably temporary surge of population movement into Shiga Prefecture exaggerates that prefecture's economic growth projection.

The biggest projected economic decline is in Nagasaki Prefecture, followed by Akita, Wakayama, Yamaguchi, Ehime, and Shizuoka prefectures. Large expected declines in the size of the workforce are the main reason for the projected economic shrinkage in Nagasaki, Akita, and Yamaguchi. The projected increases in labor productivity are comparatively high in those prefectures. In contrast, an aging workforce and a resultant decline in labor productivity are the main reason for the projected economic shrinkage in Shizuoka. The expected decline in the size of the workforce is relatively small in that prefecture.

Our projections for four prefectures and regions—Tokyo, Hanshin, Shizuoka, and Ibaraki—show declines in labor productivity, and the expected increases in labor productivity are exceedingly small in Tochigi, Nara, Kyoto, Chukyo, Hiroshima, Yamanashi, and Gunma. Aging workforces will thus depress labor productivity unavoidably in Japan's three largest metropolitan areas and in the nation's other urban regions. Even continuing inflows of population, reflected in figure 24, and continuing technological advances will be insufficient to offset the effects of that aging. The economies of Japan's most-urbanized regions will thus shrink sharply despite relatively small declines in the size of their workforces.

Of the prefectures and regions cited in the preceding paragraph, the projected economic shrinkage exceeds the national average in Ibaraki, Tochigi, Hanshin, Nara, and Hiroshima, and it basically matches the national average in the others. These are the very prefectures and regions whose economic vitality has driven Japan's economic growth and development. So their coming slowdown marks a profound change in Japan's economic cartography.

Of some interest is the projected lack of significant economic shrinkage in Miyagi, Fukuoka, and Kagoshima prefectures. The reason for their economic steadiness is clear in the graphs: minimal shrinkage in the workforce in Miyagi and Fukuoka and a strong rise in labor productivity in Kagoshima.

Figure 26 helps explain the regional diversity in economic trends. It shows the composition of population by age in the Tokyo region and in four selected prefectures in 2000 and 2030. As in figure 24, the data here includes the assumption of continuing population movement at the present pace and pattern. The two vertical dotted lines delineate the 20–54 age range, where labor productivity is generally high.

We have seen that labor productivity will decline in the Tokyo region, and a big reason for that decline is evident in figure 26. The upper graph shows that residents in their 20s and 30s account for an extremely high

Figure 24a

Change in Prefectural Income from 1998 to 2030: Assuming Population Movement

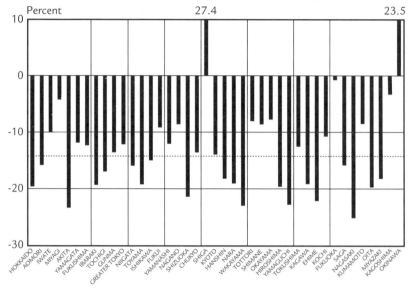

Figure 24b

Factors in the Change in Prefectural Income

Rise or Decline in Labor Productivity ("labor productivity" defined as prefectural income per working person)

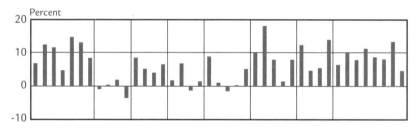

Increase or Decrease in Workforce

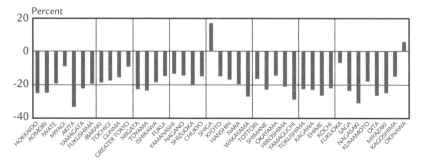

Sources: Prefectural economic data published by the Economic Planning Agency
   (now part of the Cabinet Office) for 1998 and projections by the author for 2030

Figure 25a

Change in Prefectural Income from 1998 to 2030: Assuming No Population Movement

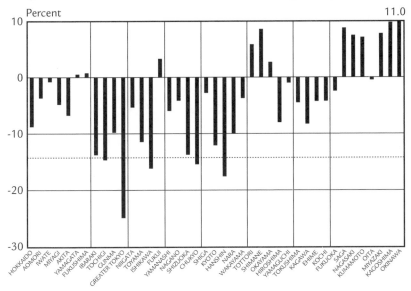

Figure 25b

Factors in the Change in Prefectural Income

Rise or Decline in Labor Productivity ("labor productivity" defined as prefectural income per working person)

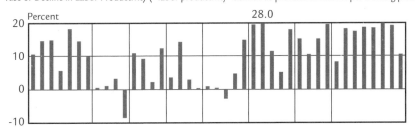

Increase or Decrease in Workforce

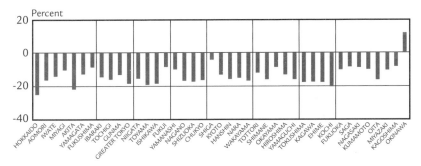

Sources: Prefectural economic data published by the Economic Planning Agency
(now part of the Cabinet Office) for 1998 and projections by the author for 2030

Figure 26

Population Composition by Age Stratum

In 2000

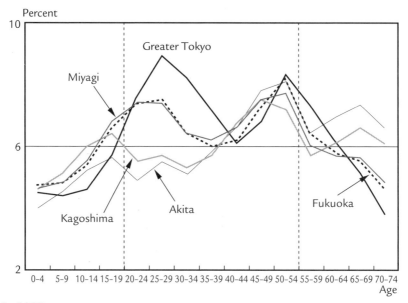

In 2030

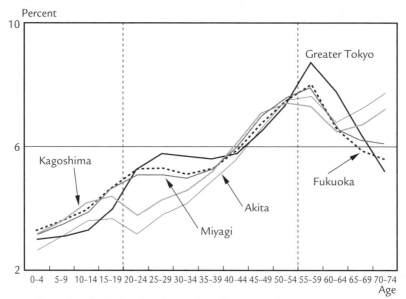

Sources: Census data for 2000 and projections by Fujimasa Iwao for 2030

proportion of the Tokyo region's population. That demographic weighting supports Tokyo's presently high labor productivity. The lower graph shows that the population in the 20-to-39 age bracket will decline sharply by 2030. That decline will occur, as noted, despite a continuing inflow of population. The aging of the workforce in the Tokyo region figures decisively in the projected decline in labor productivity there.

Kagoshima Prefecture presents a contrasting example. Outflows of population have greatly reduced the percentage of the population in the 20-to-39 age bracket there. So the upper age bracket in the workforce will not increase greatly as a percentage of the total. Meanwhile, a high birthrate (1.66 in 1995) will moderate the decline of the high-productivity age bracket as a percentage of the total workforce. These factors will prevent substantial change in the age profile of the workforce in Kagoshima. Technological advances, therefore, will translate directly into gains in labor productivity. Similar factors account for the projected gains in labor productivity indicated in figure 24 for Shimane, Kochi, Tokushima, Aomori, Iwate, Akita, and Yamagata prefectures.

An earlier pattern of population outflows will thus soften the adverse economic effects of aging and population decline in several prefectures. Those prefectures are harbingers for the economic tribulations that demographic change will occasion in Japan's three largest metropolises and in other urbanized regions of the nation. Those issues will present the biggest challenges in the biggest metropolises because the declining inflows of young people will amplify their effect. But similar trends will be evident in smaller urban centers, such as Miyagi and Fukuoka prefectures.

Labor productivity will increase less in Miyagi and in Fukuoka than in Kagoshima Prefecture, for example, but the shrinkage of their workforces will be modest. That is because Miyagi and Fukuoka, like Tokyo, have a lot of young workers who will still be working in 2030. To be sure, the percentage of young people in the workforces of those two prefectures is lower than in the Tokyo region. But the birthrate is higher in Miyagi (1.46) and in Fukuoka (1.45) than in Tokyo, and those prefectures consequently have higher percentages of young people who will enter the workforce. The overall percentage declines in their workforces will therefore be comparable to the small decline in Tokyo.

Population outflows will have an especially telling effect on the economy of Akita Prefecture. Outflows of population are an issue throughout the northern part of the main Japanese island of Honshu, and Akita has the highest departure rate in the region. Its economy is therefore likely to shrink substantially despite strong growth in labor productivity. Akita's economic shrinkage is likely to be comparable to that of Nagasaki Prefecture, on the southerly island of Kyushu.

THE FORECASTS: (2) ASSUMING NO POPULATION MOVEMENT

Let's examine what the economic prospects for Japan's prefectures and regions look like when we assume no population movement. This assumption is to account for the possibility that population movements will not continue at their recent pace and pattern. That possibility warrants consideration for several reasons. Economic shrinkage, for example, will occasion changes in corporate behavior and in personal behavior. Consumption patterns and lifestyles will presumably change as continuing gains in income become less reliable, and people's priorities in choosing employment will presumably change, too. The implications of these and other developments are debatable. What is all but certain, however, is that regional differentials in wages and salaries will narrow.

The chief determinant of wage and salary levels is labor productivity. Value-added generated per worker determines the amount of money available for employee compensation. Two other factors that affect wage and salary levels are (1) labor supply and demand and (2) the comparative strength of employers and labor unions. The comparative strength of corporate management relative to organized labor has depressed wage and salary levels in Japan, as we have seen. Nonetheless, labor productivity has remained the chief reference criterion for wages and salaries. Labor productivity in Japan is highest in the Tokyo region and in the nation's other large metropolitan areas. That has supported the highest wage and salary levels in the nation, and it has attracted heavy concentrations of population.

We can thus discuss labor productivity in terms of personal income levels. Average annual per capita income in Japan outside the nation's three largest metropolitan areas was ¥5,230,000 in 1998. In contrast, it was ¥6,600,000 in the Tokyo region, ¥5,800,000 in Chukyo, and ¥6,320,000 in Hanshin. We saw in figure 24, however, that labor productivity in the three main metropolitan areas will decline or increase only minimally in the years to 2030 and that it will rise substantially, on average, elsewhere in the nation. In 2030, our projections for average annual income per capita, assuming continued population movement at recent rates, are ¥6,390,000 in Tokyo, ¥5,890,000 in Chukyo, ¥6,230,000 in Hanshin, and ¥5,560,000 in other regions of Japan. The average income level outside the three largest metropolitan areas would thus reach 87.0% of the Tokyo level, up from only 79.2% in 1998.

The narrowing of income differentials will presumably diminish the motivation for young people to move to Japan's large metropolises. That would result in even-faster aging of the metropolitan workforces and would lower labor productivity and wage and salary levels, which would further diminish the metropolises' appeal. We cannot predict precisely how far this feedback loop will progress, but we can be reasonably certain that population movement will not continue at the pace of recent years. Population distribution will presumably be somewhere between the projection based on the extension of recent trends and the projection based on the assumption of no population movement. Economic performance in each region will also presumably be somewhere between the projections based on the two assumptions.

A combination of the two assumptions about population movement will therefore be a useful basis for projecting economic trends. Assuming no population movement (figure 25) produces strikingly different projections from what results from assuming continued population movement at the recent pace (figure 24). We see sharp economic shrinkage in Japan's large metropolitan areas and strong economic growth—or at least much less economic shrinkage—in the other regions of the nation. Growth is notably strong in Tottori, Shimane, and Okinawa prefectures. It is also strong in most of the prefectures of Kyushu: Kagoshima, Miyazaki, Kumamoto, Nagasaki, and Saga. The only two Kyushu prefectures where projected economic growth is negative when we assume no population movement are Oita and Fukuoka, and the shrinkage in Oita is much smaller than when we assume continued population movement at the recent rate. Only highly urbanized and industrialized Fukuoka shows greater economic shrinkage when we assume no population movement.

The prefectures that have suffered the largest exoduses of young people naturally show the greatest economic improvement when we assume the cessation of that trend. Their assumed workforces become younger and, augmented by technological advances, support higher labor productivity. The declines in the size of their workforces, meanwhile, are smaller. These factors yield a huge, positive difference in economic growth.

A PRONOUNCED NARROWING OF REGIONAL ECONOMIC DISPARITY

Economic shrinkage in Japan's three largest metropolitan areas is all but certain to be larger than the national average. That is apparent when we forecast economic growth based on the assumption of more population movement than assumed in figure 25 (no population movement) and less than assumed in figure 24 (continued population movement at the same rate as in recent years). Economic shrinkage could be especially large in Tokyo if and as population inflows slow. Other regions where economic shrinkage appears likely to exceed the national average are Hokkaido, Akita, Ibaraki, Tochigi, Toyama, Ishikawa, Shizuoka, and Nara prefectures. We can expect to see economic expansion in Shiga, Kagoshima, and Okinawa prefectures, and we can expect the prefectural economies of Tottori, Shimane, Fukuoka, and Kumamoto to at least retain their present scale.

Population shrinkage and aging are about to achieve something that Japan's economic policy makers were unable to achieve: regional economic equality. Equilibrium in economic development has long been the stated goal of Japanese government policy. It has been the centerpiece of the five comprehensive national development plans adopted by the government since 1962. But despite the government's best efforts, regional economic disparity has only broadened. Now, changing demographics promise to bring about the hitherto unattainable goal of regional equilibrium. And that would only underline the impotence of government policy.

AN UNSUSTAINABLE STRUCTURE OF LABOR

Some readers will assert that the Tokyo region and Japan's two other largest metropolitan areas will retain their present industrial structure and their high labor productivity. Japan's largest metropolitan areas, they will insist, will continue to attract labor from throughout the nation. Workers suitable for highly mechanized industry will continue to converge on the

Figure 27

Concentration of Population in Greater Tokyo

The solid lines for the years after 2000 are for projected population assuming population movement. The dotted lines indicate the increases that would be necessary to maintain a constant age demographic in the workforce.

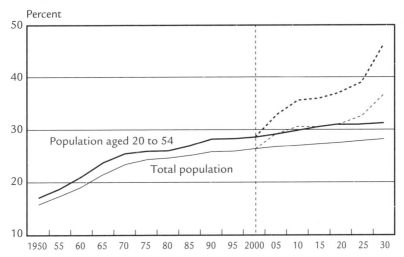

Percent

Population aged 20 to 54

Total population

1950 55 60 65 70 75 80 85 90 95 2000 05 10 15 20 25 30

Sources: Census data for the years to 2000 and calculations by the author for subsequent years

metropolitan areas, readers will object, and they will come in sufficient numbers to maintain the present level of industrial activity.

Let's deal with this counterargument by taking a look at how big an inflow of population it implicitly assumes. Even if population movement continues at its recent pace, workers aged 20 to 54 will number only about 13.3 million in the Tokyo region in 2030. An additional inflow of some 6.3 million people in that age bracket would be necessary to maintain the present age structure of the workforce. The dotted lines in figure 27 show what that would mean for the Tokyo region's share of the national population. Those lines express the percentage of the total population and the percentage of the 20-to-54 population. Their divergence from the solid lines, which reflect continued population movement at recent rates, demonstrates the implausibility of the scenario.

Even more daunting are the absolute numbers. The population inflow under discussion would increase the Tokyo region's population 23.0%, to 41.1 million in 2030, from 33.4 million in 2000. Real estate prices alone would be sufficient to prevent that kind of population shift. As if further evidence was necessary, the implications for wage and salary levels are also convincing. Companies are wholly unlikely to pay the escalating compensation that would be necessary to attract the increased inflows of labor. Industry in the Tokyo region is far more likely to adapt to the changing demographics of the workforce there—by modifying production systems and by shifting to different industrial sectors. That might entail accepting lower levels of labor productivity, but it will support higher levels of corporate profitability.

Corporate mobility

Another likely objection to the author's arguments is the long-standing decline of industrial activity outside Japan's metropolitan regions. Some readers will note that industry has generally withered outside those regions since World War II and that numerous companies have abandoned the countryside. Those readers will suggest that the slowing or even a reversal of demographic aging will be counterproductive. A shortage of employment opportunities, they will argue, will prompt more people to leave for the metropolitan areas.

The answer to this objection is Japan's impending shift to a consumption-led economy, as discussed in chapter 2. We have seen that Japanese industry concentrated in the nation's metropolitan areas and abandoned the countryside after World War II. We have seen, too, that investment-oriented government policy drove that concentration. Investment has long accounted for a larger share of the economy in Japan than in any other large industrialized nation. And investment has concentrated more in Japan than in other nations on capital goods sectors.

Japanese investment has concentrated especially on large-scale, capital-intensive manufacturing, such as steel, nonferrous metals, ceramics, heavy electrical equipment, and heavy machinery. That manufacturing relies almost entirely on imports for its raw materials, so corporations have needed to build their plants near large deepwater ports. The manufacturing also requires extensive tracts of land for its sprawling plant complexes. In Japan, the venues that fulfill these conditions are precisely the Tokyo, Nagoya, and Hanshin metropolitan areas.

Industry thus concentrated in Japan's three largest metropolises at the expense of other regions in the nation. And investment increased sharply as a share of total private-sector demand. Investment accounted for 27.0% of private-sector demand in 1972, just before the first oil crisis, compared with 9.4% in 1955.

In the years ahead, investment in Japan will decline, and consumption will increase. Consumer goods industries will grow and develop. And those industries will not necessarily require coastal sites for their manufacturing activity or for their raw materials purchasing. They will also differ from capital goods industries in the way they allocate their production resources. Capital goods industries have concentrated production at large plants and shipped their products throughout the nation. Consumer goods industries will tend to distribute their production widely and manufacture goods near centers of demand.

Japan's three largest metropolitan areas, of course, are huge centers of demand for consumer goods. Those goods, however, tend increasingly to require sophisticated manufacturing, and securing skilled labor for that manufacturing will become progressively difficult in the metropolitan areas. That is another factor that will promote a broad geographical distribution of manufacturing. We might even witness the development of production centers for different categories of consumer goods in different parts of Japan.

Labor in postwar Japan has traditionally gravitated to the sites of corporate activity. That has been because capital goods manufacturers, the core of Japanese industry, have operated at a limited number of venues. It is also because those manufacturers have pursued huge economies of scale, which has occasioned a large geographical movement of labor. That has sapped Japan's outlying regions of labor and enervated their industries. The resultant concentration of population between 1950 and 1970 is evident in figure 27.

Japan's shrinking-population economy will increasingly oblige companies to move to where labor is available. That will raise incomes in regions outside the main metropolitan centers, and it will heighten the appeal of those regions as markets. Employment opportunities are therefore likely to increase, rather than decrease, in Japan's outlying prefectures. So the notion of insufficient employment in those regions stimulating continued migration to the large metropolitan areas seems implausible.

GROWING AFFLUENCE IN THE COUNTRYSIDE: NARROWING DIFFERENTIALS IN LIVING STANDARDS

PER CAPITA INCOME: UP IN THE NONMETROPOLITAN PREFECTURES, DOWN IN THE METROPOLITAN AREAS

We have seen that the population will shrink in nearly every region of Japan over the years to 2030 and that population shrinkage will mean economic shrinkage. The economic indicator that commands our attention, however, is per capita income. That indicator, rather than GDP, is what determines living standards.

Projections for the percentage change in per capita income from 1998 to 2030 in each prefecture and region of Japan appear in figure 28. The figure rebuts the oft-heard assertion that population shrinkage and aging will affect Japan's nonmetropolitan prefectures more than the nation's metropolitan centers. It indicates inevitable declines in the average standard of living in Japan's three largest metropolitan areas and in some of their neighboring prefectures. Especially striking is the sharp decline in per capita income in the Tokyo region. That decline is even sharper than the declines for the Tokyo region in figures 24 and 25. Those figures depicted change in per capita income as change in labor productivity. But aging in the Tokyo region will greatly reduce the economically active percentage of the population. So average per capita income in the population at large will decline precipitously, as shown in figure 28.

We also see declines in per capita income in figure 28 for the Hanshin and Chukyo metropolitan areas and for the Tokyo neighbors Ibaraki and Tochigi prefectures. Per capita income will decline in those regions and prefectures regardless of whether we assume continued population movement or no population movement.

Figure 28 indicates declines in per capita income for Hokkaido, Shizuoka, Kyoto, Nara, and Hiroshima prefectures when we assume a continued movement of population. It indicates increases or only a nominal decline in per capita income for those prefectures, however, when we assume no population movement. Change in the pattern of population movement, therefore, could enable those prefectures to maintain their

Figure 28

Percent Change in Per Capita Prefectural Income from 1998 to 2030

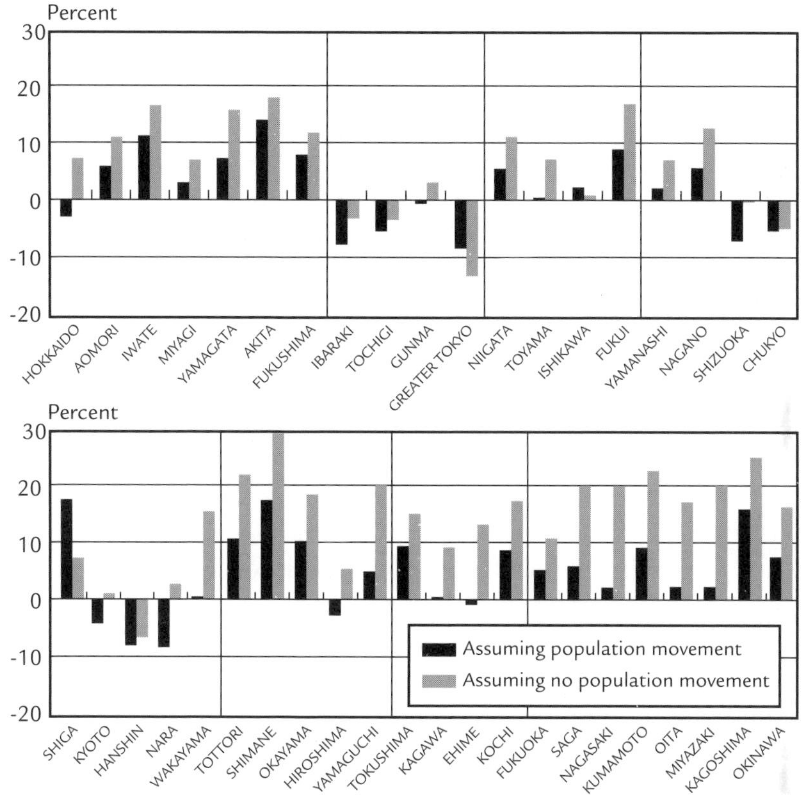

Percent

Percent

Assuming population movement
Assuming no population movement

Sources: Prefectural economic data published by the Economic Planning Agency (now part of the Cabinet Office) for 1998 and projections by the author for 2030

present standards of living or to at least minimize the declines.

Figure 28 indicates gains in living standards for Japan's nonmetro-politan prefectures, with or without population movement. Some of the prefectures, however, show large differentials in growth in per capita income depending on our assumption about population movement. That is because of the large outflows of population in recent years. Actual gains in per capita income and in living standards will thus depend on the pace of the decentralization of Japanese industry.

We also need to keep in mind the presently substantial differentials in per capita income and in living standards between Japan's large metropolitan areas and the nation's other regions. To suggest that the outlying regions will become even more affluent than the metropolitan centers would be rash. We can be certain, however, that the differentials will narrow.

The gap between Japan's most-affluent region, the Tokyo metropolitan area, and its least-affluent regions, Okinawa and Kagoshima, was extremely large in 1998. As indexes of the Tokyo level, per capita income was 60.2 in Okinawa and 63.7 in Kagoshima. Our projections call for those figures to rise to 70.8 and 80.7 by 2030, assuming continued population movement at the recent rate, and to 80.8 and 91.8, assuming no population movement.

Tokyo will remain among the most-affluent regions in Japan in 2030 if population movement continues. Our projections call for Tokyo to have the second-highest per capita income in the nation, after Shiga Prefecture, assuming continued population movement. Tokyo's projected per capita income ranks only 12th among the 41 prefectures and regions cited, however, when we assume no population movement.

The total absence of population movement is, of course, an extreme and unrealistic assumption. But we can see that a pronounced narrowing of the differential in per capita income and in living standards between Tokyo and Japan's other regions is inevitable. The pursuit of higher living standards in the postwar era has led Japanese to Tokyo and to Japan's other large metropolitan areas. Now, regions throughout the nation will offer opportunities for gains in living standards. Population shrinkage and aging thus promise to shape a happier society for Japan.

A BUMPY ROAD AHEAD

Although change in the structure of labor and in the structure of demand will help narrow the regional economic differentials in Japan, policy makers will need to address other daunting issues to fundamentally revitalize prefectural economies throughout the nation. Those economies rely heavily on subsidies from the national government, including huge public works spending and distributions of tax revenues. Japan's public works spending will decline sharply, however, and declining tax revenues in Japan's three largest metropolises will reduce the pool of funds available for regional subsidies.

In addition, the outlying prefectures' prospective new industries will encounter intense competition from their counterparts in the metropolitan regions. Attaining technological competitiveness amid the mounting sophistication of production processes and of product specifications will be a huge challenge. Another concern is whether the deteriorating industries in several prefectures will survive long enough to reap the benefits of the changing structures of labor and of demand.

Japan's road to regional revitalization will thus have plenty of bumps along the way. The economic decline that has occurred in prefectures throughout the nation has occurred despite determined efforts in those prefectures. So regional economic management is a challenging task at best. On the other hand, regional economic decline has resulted partly from ill-conceived policies. Sounder economic management is possible as policy makers learn from the mistakes of the past. And to repeat, the sweeping environmental change wrought by population shrinkage and aging will yield immense opportunities for prefectures throughout Japan. We will examine the policy options for Japan's nonmetropolitan prefectures in chapter 6.

CHAPTER IV

Smaller Government: Rethinking Public Services

Population shrinkage and aging focus attention on government policy, especially on fiscal policy. Government policy is a crucial variable in the pattern of change wrought by evolving demographics in corporate management, in regional economic management, and in the lifestyles of the citizenry. Future benefits and contributions under the national pension program receive a lot of attention as crucial factors in people's financial planning. But other aspects of fiscal and social policy, both at the national level and at the local level, are influential considerations in personal lifestyles and in corporate management. The outlook for public works spending, for example, warrants careful attention. Public works projects create the infrastructure for personal lifestyles and for industrial activity. They also account for a big part of the demand for Japan's capital goods industries.

We will take a close look at the likely effect of population shrinkage and aging on personal lifestyles in chapter 5. Here, we will examine what demographic change will mean for the national pension program, for public works projects, and for taxation and fiscal expenditures.

Japan's Unsustainable Pension Program

Pensions at a Turning Point

The aging of the population changes the basic context of the national pension program. As we saw in figure 8 (page 25), the economically

103

active percentage of the Japanese population will decline precipitously. The nonworking percentage of the population will thus increase sharply. So maintaining individual pension benefits at the present level would mean a big increase in individual contributions. Conversely, maintaining contributions at the present level would entail a big cut in benefits.

Problems for the pension program are an inevitable result of population aging, and the impending aging of the Japanese population was clear by the 1970s. But only recently has the outlook for the national pension program become a hot issue. A possible reason for the slow awakening to this issue is evident in figure 8: The economically active percentage of the population had not changed much from the 1970s until recently. More working women and other factors combined to prevent a decline in the economically active percentage of the population despite overall aging. That forestalled the need for adjusting pension benefits or contributions, and it presumably delayed the national awakening to the problem at hand. Now, the rapid pace of aging will unavoidably reduce the economically active percentage of the population. That will happen even if the already-high percentage of working women rises further. Japan's national pension program, in other words, is at a turning point.

Let's take a look at the fiscal outlook for the pension program. Comprehensive data about the program, however, is unavailable to the public. We lack a sufficient basis, for example, to make separate projections for the twin pillars of the public pension system: Employees' Pension Insurance and the National Pension system. So we will make our projections on the basis of the system of national accounts.

Statistical limitations, meanwhile, oblige us to deal with revenues and expenditures as totals for the public pension program and the national health insurance program. This latter consideration, however, does not diminish the significance of our projections. Our primary concern here is the fiscal effect of a shrinking and aging population on Japan's social insurance programs overall. And the aging of the population is the chief reason for the projected increase in medical expenditures.

Figure 29 presents past and future expenditures and revenue from contributions under Japan's principal social insurance programs. The author has projected future benefits and contributions on the assumption that individual benefits remain at their present level and that contributions, as a percentage of personal income, also remain constant. Note

Figure 29

Expenditures and Contributions in Japan's Principal Social Insurance Programs

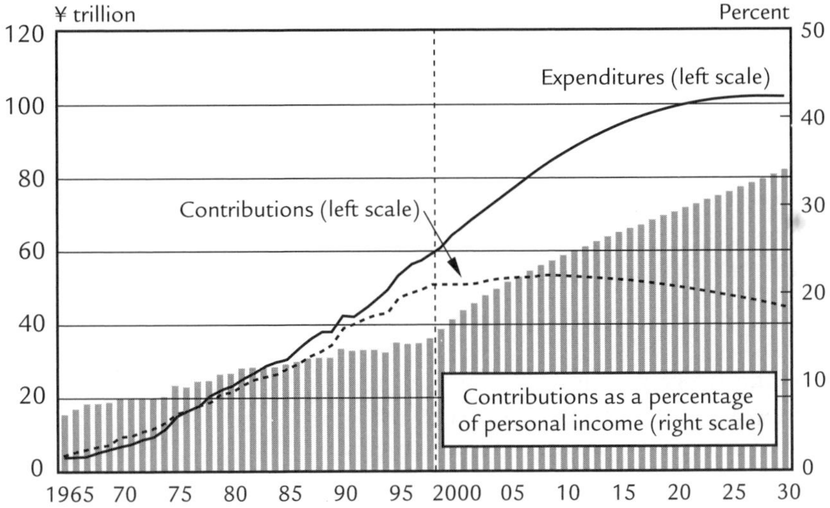

Sources: National accounts data published by the Japanese government for the years to 1998 and projections by the author for subsequent years

that the expenditures continue to grow for the entire time frame of the graph, though the pace of growth slows after 2020. Real (inflation-adjusted) expenditures increase more than 70%, to ¥101.7 trillion in 2030, from ¥59.4 trillion in 1998. Revenues from contributions, however, edge up only slightly from 1998 to 2010 and then begin to decline.

The funding shortfall in Japan's social insurance programs would thus swell annually, to ¥33.4 trillion in 2010 and to ¥57.0 trillion in 2030, from ¥8.7 trillion in 1998. Contributions would cover only 44.0% of expenditures under the programs in 2030. The cumulative shortfall for the years from 1998 to 2030 would total ¥1,240 trillion. To put that total in perspective, it is roughly equivalent to aggregate personal financial assets in Japan today.

Maintaining benefits at their present level and funding them fully with contributions would entail a sharp rise in contribution rates. The vertical bars in figure 29 indicate contributions to Japan's social insurance programs as a percentage of personal income. That percentage more than doubles, to 34.0% in 2030, from 15.0% in 1998. Maintaining benefits at the present level is thus a daunting proposition, at best. On the other hand, maintaining contributions at their present percentage of personal income while balancing the social insurance programs would mean a huge reduction in benefits. The benefits per person in 2030 would be less than half, 44%, of the benefits in 1998.

THE GOVERNMENT'S EXTREMELY UNREALISTIC REFORM PROPOSALS

Japan's social insurance programs had a reserve of ¥244.6 trillion in 1998. That reserve is a legacy of the funding format employed originally for the pension program. Today's pay-as-you-go pension funding, in which contributions by working people pay for benefits to retirees, produces no reserve. But the program originally used an accumulative contribution format, in which people saved for their retirement. The reserve on hand is what remains from that format. It allowed for maintaining pension benefits and contributions at basically constant levels after Japan's social insurance programs slipped into deficit in the late 1970s and even after the deficits began broadening notably in the 1990s.

Only a government could get away with tearing up people's savings agreements and with using the savings for other purposes. Be that as it may, the accumulated reserve also served to delay the general awakening to the pension program's problems.

The author calculates that Japan's pension program will deplete its reserve completely by 2009. Unless the government resorts to debt funding for the program, it will need to reduce benefits, increase contributions, or use some combination of both. The funding shortfall under the present scheme has already begun to widen rapidly, as seen in figure 29. Belatedly recognizing the problem, the government prepared a set of "reforms," which the Diet passed in 2004. The proposed changes, however, reveal a woefully inadequate grasp of the severity of the problem.

Under the government's changes, individual contributions as a percentage of personal income will increase 35% by 2017, and benefits will decline 16% by 2022. The government asserts that those changes will be sufficient to balance the program. According to the author's calculations, the government's proposed changes will reduce the program's accumulated deficit in 2030 only about one-half, to ¥609 trillion. Even drawing on everything left in the program's reserve will still leave the accumulated deficit at ¥470 trillion.

The author calculates that maintaining benefits at the level proposed by the government would necessitate increasing the average contribution rate 72% by 2017 and that maintaining the average contribution rate at the level proposed by the government would necessitate reducing benefits 37%. Our figures for social insurance revenues and outlays, as noted, include health insurance, as well as pension insurance. Even discounting for that distortion, the government's proposals are wholly inadequate to balance the pension insurance portion of the social insurance program. The author, incidentally, has assumed a constant level of health insurance expenditures per person in preparing these projections. In practice, those expenditures could well rise as a result of increasingly sophisticated medical treatment and of the aging of the population. And that would further broaden the funding gap in Japan's social insurance program.

We can only guess at the reasons for the imbalance between revenues and outlays in the government's reform proposals. That is because the government has not revealed details of the assumptions that underlie its calculations. It has presumably employed higher figures than the author has for the economically active percentage of the population and for the economic growth rate. The author's assumptions for both of those factors, however, are on the high side of the reasonable range of expectations. As noted in chapter 2, the author has assumed that the female percentage of Japan's work force will continue to increase at the recent rate until 2030, and he has assumed the highest theoretically possible rate of economic growth. We must assume that the government's reform proposals rest on wholly unrealistic assumptions.

EXTREME EQUALITY

The optimal levels of benefits and contributions in Japan's public pension program should be up to the Japanese people to decide. To promote public discourse and sound decisions, the government should freely disclose important information about the pension program. The discourse needs to begin, however, with careful consideration of the proper role of public pensions in a shrinking and aging society.

Public pensions are the ultimate in social equalizing. The story of modern social development in Japan is a tale of increasing social equality. Japan began holding democratic elections, and it subsequently adopted universal suffrage. The principle of equal opportunity took hold in Japan. Public pensions extend that principle into the realm of equal results: people receive enough money to live even when they are no longer working. Society takes responsibility for ensuring the livelihoods of people who have grown too old to work.

Making Japan's pension program possible were economic growth and the resultant dramatic rise in personal incomes. People began to earn more than they required for immediate needs, and that gave society the financial wherewithal to care for the nonworking elderly. The sustainability of that arrangement depended, however, on avoiding an inordinate increase in nonworking elderly relative to the working population. A continuing relative increase in nonworking elderly would impose a growing burden on working people and would crimp their standard of living. To ascertain the sustainability of the pension program, we thus need to examine two factors: the numerical balance between nonworking elderly and working people and trends in personal incomes.

Figure 30 presents projected trends in the number of elderly people in Japan, the number of working-age people, and the ratio of those two numbers. The numbers of elderly people and working-age people in Japan displayed similar trends until recently, and the ratio of elderly to working-age people rose only slightly. That ratio will now surge as the number of elderly continues to grow and as the working-age population shrinks rapidly. In 2000, three working people in Japan supported a single pensioner. By 2014, two working people will need to support each pensioner, and by 2030, each pensioner will depend on only 1.5 working people. We will examine the outlook for incomes closely in the next chapter, and a summary of the author's projections for incomes appears there in figure 33 (page 133). So we will confine our discussion of incomes here to a few essential considerations. Per capita income for working people in Japan rose 2.4-fold between 1970 and 2000, but the author projects that it will rise only 9.1% over the 30 years from 2000 to 2030. That increase is utterly insufficient to allow for maintaining benefits and contributions in Japan's public pension program at their present levels.

Reducing benefits would reinforce the sustainability of the pension program. Japanese have traditionally expected their pension benefits, however, to be sufficient for pensioners to live on. They would not easily countenance a reduction in benefits below the level necessary to support

Figure 30
Japan's Elderly Population and Working-Age Population

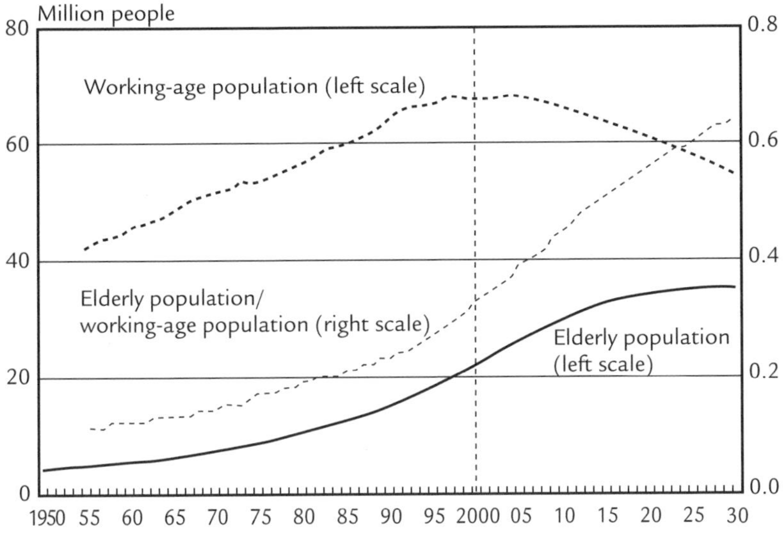

Sources: National accounts data and census data published by the Japanese government for the years to 2000 and projections by the author for subsequent years

a reasonably comfortable standard of living. That is presumably why the government reduced benefits only 16% in its pension reforms. Meanwhile, increasing contributions enough to realistically ensure pension program sustainability would have imposed a politically unacceptable burden on working people. So the government apparently fudged by adopting unrealistically high assumptions for the economically active percentage of the population and for economic growth.

A PENSION PROGRAM FOR A SHRINKING, AGING SOCIETY

Anyone can see the impossibility of maintaining benefits at a level high enough for pensioners to live on comfortably while keeping the burden on working-age people at a viable level. The shrinking and aging of society mandate a thorough reappraisal of the role of pensions.

Think of an elderly parent who lives on remittances from his or her three grown children. And think what would happen in the unhappy event of a death among the children. The parent would be unlikely to demand a 50% increase in remittances from the two surviving children. More likely, he or she would find ways to make do on the reduced income. That is exactly what will need to happen in Japan's shrinking and aging society.

Japanese have tended to regard benefits as a constant in the pension equation and contributions as a variable. The assumption has been that contributions need to increase as necessary to keep benefits high enough to live on. New demographic realities, however, call for reversing this logic. Japanese need to determine the maximum burden that working-age people can bear and then calculate the benefits that will be payable. That is the only way to ensure the sustainability of the pension program.

In fact, the shrinking and aging of society eliminate the need for maintaining the pension program in its present form. Japan's pension program has been an alternative to encouraging people to save independently for their retirement. A justification for that approach is that pensions allow for sharing the benefits of economic growth across generations. When incomes are rising steadily, preceding generations have less money to put aside for retirement than succeeding generations do. A pay-as-you-go pension program allows for sharing the nation's growing affluence with the previous generation. That helps reduce intergenerational differentials in postretirement living standards. And it is only fair, since the efforts of the previous generation laid the economic foundation for the affluence of the following generation.

Incomes stop rising, however, in a shrinking and aged society. Society no longer has growing affluence for sharing retroactively across generations, so fairness ceases to be an issue in structuring the pension program. A response that warrants consideration is a return to a system in which people save for their own retirement. That would allow for maintaining benefits without imposing a progressively higher burden on successive generations.

Paying pension benefits out of the pensioners' own contributions superficially resembles leaving the responsibility for saving up to individuals. However, Japanese individuals left to their own devices would accumulate excessive savings. Most people expect or hope to live longer than the average. They would therefore put aside more for retirement than actual average longevity in Japanese society justifies. As we saw on page 46, excessive accumulation diminishes economic activity. It reduces consumption and thus undermines demand. A program in which people save for their own retirement would optimize accumulation by matching it to actual average longevity.

Some people suggest that relying on private-sector pension insurance would be preferable to operating a public program. The most-affluent members of society, however, would not necessarily take part in a voluntary pension program. They have ample liquidity to enjoy retirement without resorting to pensions. Pension insurance in which only the less-affluent members of society took part would be of questionable viability as a private-sector enterprise. The government could require everyone to secure pension insurance, but that would entail all sorts of inefficiencies.

Japanese need to take all these considerations into account and devise a pension format suited to their shrinking and aging society. And they need to start by recognizing that the present format, including its fundamental conceptual basis, is no longer appropriate.

THE ROLE OF PUBLIC INFRASTRUCTURE IN SUPPORTING THE ELDERLY

Any changes in Japan's public pension program will need to accommodate the people who are already receiving pensions and people who will soon become pensioners. The present pension format has been a "given" for those people in their financial planning. A sudden change in the program that entailed a substantial reduction in benefits would be unforgivably cruel. Some observers who disagree note an upward trend in the number of people who continue working into old age. That trend, they suggest, obviates the need for pension benefits at the present level. People who freely choose to continue working after turning 65 are one thing; casting old people into the workforce as a condition for their survival is something else again. Robbing people of promised pension benefits would be hideously unfair.

One promising tool for insulating pensioners and soon-to-be pensioners from the effects of changes in the pension program is housing policy. Quality, low-rent public housing would be a boon to pensioners who do not own their homes. Rent accounts for a big part of the monthly living expenses for those people. So supplying a large volume of the kind of housing described could greatly offset the effects of reduced pension benefits. It would also be fiscally efficient. Although the massive residential construction required would entail large initial investment, the housing would serve several generations of residents. It could therefore reduce the net fiscal burden on society over the long term.

Europe encountered the issue of aging populations before Japan did, and public housing has been instrumental in ensuring stable livelihoods for the elderly in several European nations. Housing in Japan, to be sure, presents special issues. The high frequency of earthquakes requires attention in building design and construction, and it also affects the expected average longevity of structures. Most of Japan is comparatively hot and humid, which is also a consideration in architectural planning. But the fact remains that buildings in Japan tend to be less durable than they could and should be. Incorporating improved technology to maximize the durability of the newly constructed public housing would minimize the fiscal cost for society.

Other measures are available to accommodate pensioners who own their homes. For example, the government—national or local—could purchase pensioners' homes. It could pay for the purchases in monthly installments calculated on the basis of average lifespan. The government would lose on pensioners who lived longer than average, and it would gain on those who died earlier than average. But the net loss and gain would be zero for the government and for the pensioners overall.

The land that came into the hands of the government through this policy could become sites for new public housing. It could also support other kinds of public facilities that will become necessary in Japan's aged society. Building those facilities will add further to the up-front fiscal cost for society, and securing sufficient funding would be an issue. Some of that funding would become available from a fundamental restructuring of Japan's public works spending. That restructuring will become necessary as Japan's economy shrinks and as the geographical distribution of economic activity in Japan shifts.

Japanese need to regard public housing as public infrastructure. Increasing and upgrading that infrastructure and putting it to good use can be effective ways of supporting the nation's elderly. This would be more than a one-time measure for offsetting the effects of changes in the pension program; housing policy would become a pillar of public policy for supporting the nation's elderly. As noted, Japan will soon have an ultra-aged society, where more than 30% of the population is older than

65. It will be unable to fund all public support for the elderly through transferring income from the working population to the nonworking population. Even switching from a pay-as-you-go pension system to a savings-accumulation system would entail pain. Lengthening lifespans mean that working-age Japanese would need to put aside growing sums to provide for retirement.

All of this is to say that the pension program alone will be inadequate to ensure a sound foundation for Japan's aged society. Japan will need to mobilize public infrastructure extensively and imaginatively. Retirees will be free to choose whether or not to avail themselves of the newly available support. But support needs to be available to people who need or want that support. Japanese harbor growing anxiety about the aging of society, and a big reason for that anxiety is the government's lack of countermeasures for aging other than pensions. The author has cited public housing as a promising sector for expanding support for the elderly. Investment in cultural facilities, in parks and plazas, and in other public facilities will also be essential. Laying a sound foundation for Japan's aged society will require more than pensions; it will also require the systematic combination of public works spending and public services.

A HALVING OF PUBLIC WORKS SPENDING

EXPANDED PUBLIC WORKS PROJECTS AS A THREAT TO THE JAPANESE ECONOMY

A diminished capacity for investment is a characteristic of a shrinking-population economy. Aging reduces the economically active percentage of the population, and the pool of national savings shrinks. That necessitates a sharp reduction in gross investment—the sum of private-sector capital spending, public works spending, housing investment, and net exports. As we have seen, Japan's gross investment is poised to shrink faster than the economy overall. The projections on page 64 suggest that gross investment in 2030 will be 19.4% less than in 2000.

Investment in Japan has hitherto been virtually free of any savings-related constraints. A strong propensity to save has generated ample savings for funding corporate investment and public works spending. Japanese public works spending expanded rapidly in the 1990s, and the capital market readily absorbed the national and local government bonds issued to finance that investment. Even though private-sector capital spending was also robust, interest rates barely rose. Savings were so immense, in other words, that the increased investment did not upset the balance of supply and demand for funds. No amount of public works spending caused a crowding-out effect in the capital markets.

Things are changing. Gross investment in Japan will encounter a strict upward limit. For the first time in living memory, Japanese will need to make choices in allocating limited investment funding. They will need to think carefully about which investment options offer the best return on investment for the nation overall.

Generalizing about the optimal distribution of investment is difficult. That is a decision for the Japanese people to make, and they will make that decision through the demand they assert through their economic activity. They might present strong demand, for example, for an airport or highway. The national government or a local government will issue bonds to finance the requisite public works spending. Banks regard the risk of default by public-sector bond issuers as minimal, and they will gladly invest in the bonds, even if that means curtailing their lending to private-sector borrowers. Private-sector companies will then need to reduce their capital spending. The weighting of public works spending in gross investment will increase, and the weighting of private-sector capital spending will decline.

We mustn't be judgmental about the rightness or wrongness of that outcome. Our basic stance in liberal economics is that the best economic system is one where people determine the allocation of investment freely through their economic activity. The outcome in our example reflects choices made by the Japanese people through the marketplace, and we must therefore regard it as the optimal economic outcome for Japan at the time. We also need to recognize, however, that the resultant decline in private-sector capital spending will diminish the Japanese economy overall. That is because public works spending contributes little to productive capacity, whereas private-sector capital spending increases productive capacity efficiently.

Note that public works spending contributed more to Japan's productive capacity in the nation's earlier stages of industrial development. When Japan lacked sufficient infrastructure to support modern industrial activity, adding infrastructure contributed directly to gains in productive capacity. Japan now has a well-developed infrastructure, however, and the incremental benefits of new airports and highways are minimal in terms of increasing productive capacity.

Underlying the projection for Japanese economic growth in figure 11 (page 34) is the assumption that private-sector capital spending will be continuously maximal—that it will take place continuously at the highest level possible for the amount of labor available. Economic growth will fall short of that projection if public works spending increases greatly and if gross private-sector capital spending dips below the trend line in figure 10 (page 32).

An issue that we encounter here is whether people understand the economic consequences of the choices they make. An airport or highway is visible, but the mechanism by which increased public works spending diminishes the economy is invisible, and few people have a grasp of that mechanism. This calls into question our liberal economic belief in the marketplace as a sound arbiter of investment distribution.

As Japan encounters new and unfamiliar limits to investment, the government needs to explain the economic ramifications of proposed public works projects. It has a responsibility to explain how increased public works spending will diminish the economy. Japanese will also need to be newly vigilant of projects undertaken for the benefit of special interests. They need to insist more strongly than ever that any public works projects be beneficial for a large cross section of the population.

THE RIGHT AMOUNT OF PUBLIC WORKS SPENDING

Let's consider how much public works spending Japan can undertake without crowding out private-sector capital spending and diminishing the economy. Our consideration will consist of determining how much public works spending is possible without compromising the economic projections in figure 11 (page 34).

We can determine the allowable amount of public works spending by subtracting elements of real gross investment (figure 10, page 32) from national savings. The first item we subtract is private-sector capital spending, since we are predicating our consideration on maximal productivity. We assume a level of housing investment sufficient to maintain present

Figure 31
Allowable Amount of Public Works Spending

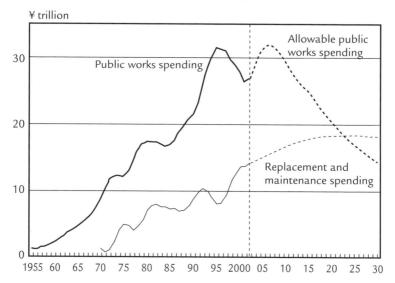

Sources: Calculations by the author on the basis of national accounts data published by
the Japanese government for the years to 2002 and projections by the author
for subsequent years

standards of living for the projected number of households. And we
assume that net exports, essential to resource-poor Japan, will conform to
their recent trend. The remainder after subtracting these items—private-
sector capital spending, housing investment, net exports—from national savings is the allowable amount of public works spending.

Figure 31 presents the results of calculating the allowable amount of
public works spending as described in the preceding paragraph. That
amount declines precipitously because of the projected decline in national savings. The amount of public works spending that will be possible in
2030 without compromising economic growth is ¥14.2 trillion. That is
down 47.0% from the actual figure of ¥26.8 trillion in 2002. Public works
spending needs to decline nearly one-half, that is, for Japan to achieve
the economic performance projected in figure 11. That would mean a
return to the level of 1976 and 1977.

We are positing a decline in public works spending that is sharper
than the projected shrinkage of the economy. Japanese might decide to
maintain a higher rate of investment in public works projects. That would

entail, as we have seen, increased economic shrinkage, and it would require a national consensus. People might accept some crowding out if they decided that the increase in infrastructure enhanced the quality of life. In any case, that is a choice that confronts the Japanese people.

THE SHOCK OF THE HALVING OF PUBLIC WORKS SPENDING

Halving Japan's public works spending would send shockwaves throughout the nation's economy. It would be an especially devastating blow to the construction industry, but it would also hit companies hard in materials sectors, such as steel and ceramics. All companies in capital goods industries that rely heavily on public-sector demand would suffer.

Profound change is in store for the structure of Japanese industry and for the relative positioning of corporations and industries, and that is only partly because of the impending reduction in public works spending. Other forces will shift the focus of the economy toward consumer demand, from investment demand, as we saw in chapter 2. But the halving of public works spending would amplify the repercussions of that shift. Public works projects account for a big proportion of the local economies of Japan's nonurban prefectures, and the effects of reduced public works spending will be notably pronounced where the dependence on that spending is highest.

The decline in public works spending will be most apparent in the quality of public infrastructure. Like private-sector plant and equipment, infrastructure has a finite lifespan and needs to be replaced periodically. It also requires continuing maintenance and repairs to maintain its structural integrity and to maintain its functional efficiency.

Spending on infrastructure renewals and maintenance has grown in step with the growth in public works spending. By the 1990s, it accounted for about 35% of total public works spending. Growth in the pool of public infrastructure will slow as public works spending declines, but spending on renewals and maintenance will need to continue rising, as shown in figure 31. All infrastructure will require maintenance, and infrastructure added during the years of rapid growth in public works spending will reach the end of its useful life and will require replacement.

The author projects that renewals and maintenance of infrastructure will account for 57.2% of public works spending in 2010 and for 90.7%

in 2020. That is assuming public works spending at the maximum level possible without crowding out private-sector capital spending and thus diminishing the economy. By 2023, spending on renewals and maintenance alone would exceed that threshold level for total public works spending. Japan will be unable to invest in any new infrastructure if it keeps public works spending within that threshold and if it conducts the required renewals and maintenance; it will be unable to conduct even the minimum required renewals and maintenance. By 2030, the threshold will decline to only 78.8% of the amount required for minimal renewals and maintenance.

Japan's infrastructure will thus begin to deteriorate, and some of it could fall into ruin. Infrastructure is, by definition, a platform for personal activity and for corporate activity. Its diminution could undermine social vitality. New York City's fiscally induced lapse of infrastructure and public services in the 1970s and 1980s was an alarming portent of what might lie ahead for Japan.

Public health and safety are also at risk. Inadequate maintenance of levees and breakwaters could invite disaster. Ill-maintained sewers would cause environmental and health problems.

Japan's public pension program and public infrastructure thus require special attention amid the shrinking and aging of the nation's population. As we have seen, sound corporate management can keep companies viable despite economic shrinkage, and that shrinkage will not cause a decline in average per capita income. But Japan's pension program and public infrastructure will soon collapse in the absence of vigorous measures to ensure their viability. Japan urgently needs to fortify its social and infrastructural support in the name of ensuring a sound foundation for its evolving society.

THE RIGHT INFRASTRUCTURE

Japan needs a completely new approach to infrastructure. Overinvestment in infrastructure, by diminishing the economy, would diminish the savings available for investment. That would further lower the maximum level of public works spending that is possible without affecting the economy adversely. It would thus reduce the potential for adding and maintaining infrastructure over the long term.

Population and economic shrinkage suggest, to be sure, that some reduction in infrastructure ought to be appropriate. But this is not to suggest that shrinkage of 10% in the population or in the economy warrants a 10% reduction in roadways or in sewage lines. The aging of society will call, on the contrary, for increases in some kinds of infrastructure, and an aged society will require new kinds of infrastructure.

Japanese need to review their infrastructure and decide which items will be essential in their shrinking and aged society. They should refrain from investing in maintenance for infrastructure deemed unnecessary or only nominally useful, and they should dispose of that infrastructure at the end of its useful life. Decisions about which infrastructure to retain and which to discard should be up to the beneficiaries of the infrastructure. The government should support sound choices by providing ample information about the social and economic changes occasioned by population shrinkage and aging and about the amount of funding available.

Japan's investment in infrastructure has hitherto taken place at the initiative of the government, and a lot of that investment has not necessarily reflected the will of the people at large. The result has been excesses in some categories of infrastructure and shortages in other categories. A more-democratic approach to allocating investment can help rectify that aberration, but people will need to accept responsibility for their choices. They will be unable to blame local or national bureaucrats for the lost benefits of infrastructure that they decided democratically to discard.

DEMOCRATIC LONG-TERM PLANNING FOR PUBLIC INFRASTRUCTURE

Fiscal considerations oblige Japanese to become increasingly selective in undertaking public works projects. Along with consuming scarce budgetary resources on a current basis, those projects necessitate increased future spending on renewals and maintenance, which further reduces the amount of funding available for new infrastructure.

Some people in Japan call for investing rapidly in infrastructure for serving future needs while funding is still available. That argument warrants some sympathy to the extent that it pertains to infrastructure that will be truly necessary. But Japanese need to regard all investment proposals in the context of the future spending that they will require on renewals and maintenance. They need to determine whether the proposed investment falls within the range of spending possible without causing adverse economic consequences.

Unfortunately, large public works projects have attracted attention as new business opportunities amid generally slow economic growth. Those projects include a preponderance of transport-related construction, such as highways, airports, and supplementary Shinkansen bullet train lines. Reducing travel time presumably yields some economic benefits. But we can only question whether all of the projects satisfy basic cost-benefit criteria. Especially worrisome is the orientation of the projects toward shortening travel times to and from Japan's three largest metropolitan areas. The impending decline in the relative importance of those areas in the Japanese economy reinforces doubts about the projects' worth.

Public works spending needs to take place in accordance with long-term planning that addresses the issues of population shrinkage and aging. That planning needs to account for the attendant increases in future spending on renewals and maintenance, and it needs to be consistent with national savings and with the optimal level of private-sector capital spending.

The rapid aging and shrinking of the Japanese population in the 21st century has been a foregone conclusion since the 1950s. That was when Japan acquired a demographic trough, as we saw in chapter 1. Economic shrinkage and the accompanying decline in capacity for investment were entirely predictable. Yet Japan still embarked on the appalling and prolonged debacle of excessive public works spending detailed in figure 31. Adopting a sound, long-term plan for public works spending surely could have prevented the worst excesses of that debacle.

Long-term planning for public works spending should be the job of local government. That will heighten people's sense of responsibility for their choices in allocating investment. And it will accommodate the increasingly local character of public works spending. An increasingly localized focus is bound to characterize public works projects amid tightening budgetary limitations.

Japan lags behind other industrialized nations in building infrastructure for supporting an aged society and for maintaining a sound environment. That is exactly the kind of infrastructure that should be subject to local decision making. Control by the central government is tantamount to securing a national consensus on issues of purely local concern. Japan should also move toward funding public works projects with local tax revenues. Project planning that is inconsistent with local tax revenues is meaningless. Establishing a linkage between local investment and local tax revenues will encourage selectivity in evaluating projects.

No Need for Tax Increases

FACTORS THAT WILL REDUCE THE NEED FOR FISCAL EXPENDITURES

We should be skeptical about the government's insistence that a tax increase will be necessary to support Japan's aged society. That is despite the undeniable need for new and expanded social welfare programs for the elderly and for new infrastructure to accommodate an older population.

An aging population, to be sure, means an increase in the number of people who are not earning incomes. That means an increase in expenditures on programs and infrastructure to care for those people. Aggravating the problem is the shift from extended families to nuclear families. A growing number of old people who formerly would have lived with their children and grandchildren will become dependents of society. Japan will need to build and operate retirement homes, nursing homes, and community centers for elderly persons. The nation will also need to develop and expand programs to support healthy and fulfilling lives for the older members of society.

Nonetheless, continuing growth in fiscal expenditures overall would be unnatural amid the shrinkage of the economy, the decline in corporate activity, and the cessation of growth in personal incomes. Overall public works spending will need to decline greatly, as we have seen, to avoid diminishing the economy unnecessarily. More than offsetting the increased investment in infrastructure required for an aged society will be decreased investment in other infrastructure.

Japan will need to manage its public works spending, including expenditures on aging-related infrastructure, within the threshold of economic viability. Some projects might receive consensus support as necessary and be worth undertaking even to the detriment of the economy overall. But economically detrimental spending is, by definition, subject to limits. Tax revenues will decline in Japan's shrinking economy even as the percentage of old people who require public assistance increases. Spending in excess of the threshold would worsen the government's fiscal condition even more than the extent of that overrun. The proposed retirement homes, community centers, and whatever would necessitate tax increases even larger than the cost of their construction.

Population shrinkage and aging will reduce the need for fiscal expenditures in lots of ways. The school-aged population—people aged 5 to 24—is likely to decline 39.4%, to 17 million in 2030, from 28 million in 2000. That will greatly reduce the need for spending on public schools and universities and for subsidies for private schools and universities. A shrinking population will presumably also occasion reductions in the size of national and local-government assemblies and in the size of government overall. The appropriate size of public spending is an issue for the people to decide. But we have every reason to believe that spending can decline overall despite the fiscal needs posed by population aging.

THE ECONOMICALLY DETRIMENTAL EFFECTS OF TAX INCREASES

Japanese need to decide how much of a tax burden they are prepared to bear to pay for public infrastructure and for social welfare programs. They need to understand that they get what they pay for: more welfare means a heavier tax burden; a lighter tax burden means less government support.

We need to be careful here to avoid making meaningless comparisons with other nations. Proponents of higher taxes, for example, like to refer to Sweden. They cite that nation as an economically and socially successful example of extensive social welfare paid for with heavy taxation. The comparison, however, is spurious. Sweden and Japan differ fundamentally in their social frameworks and value systems. Simply comparing figures for tax rates and welfare outlays in two such different nations sheds little light on the right course for Japan.

Japanese need to determine the right levels of taxation and social welfare for their nation on the basis of their own circumstances. And they need to understand that raising taxes threatens to amplify the shrinkage of Japan's economy. We saw in chapter 2 that the blind pursuit of economic growth can have unwelcome repercussions. The economic growth rate is a central consideration, however, in any discussion of tax revenues and fiscal outlays. We therefore need to come to terms with the economic ramifications of tax increases in a shrinking-population economy.

The savings rate in Japan will decline sharply in the years ahead. Japan will lack sufficient liquidity to satisfy the demand for funds for investment, as we have seen. A tax increase would deplete individuals' and corporations' liquidity further. Accompanied by a corresponding reduction in public works spending, that would not reduce the funding available for private-sector capital spending. But a tax increase would be unnecessary if a corresponding reduction in public works spending were an option. We must assume that a tax increase and the accompanying decline in savings rates would depress private-sector capital spending below the level indicated in figure 10 (page 32). And that would cause the economy to shrink even more than the author has projected.

Tax increases did not reduce the private sector's capacity for capital spending during Japan's years of continuing economic expansion. That was because individuals and corporations retained ample liquidity to channel into savings. The direct linkage between tax increases and reduced capacity for private-sector capital spending is another characteristic of a shrinking and aged society. A tax increase reduces the amount of funding available for capital spending. If companies seek to continue investing at the same pace as before the tax increase, interest rates rise. That lowers return on investment, and corporations therefore curtail their capital spending.

An alternative to raising personal and corporate income taxes would be an increase in Japan's consumption tax (a national sales tax, presently 5%). That might seem likely to affect capital spending less adversely than would an increase in the corporate tax rate. The reduction in overall savings would be about the same, however, whether it happened entirely in the consumer sector or in both the consumer and corporate sectors.

Japanese thus need to avoid tax increases altogether if they want to avoid aggravating economic shrinkage. If they want to expand public services, they should reduce spending on public works projects. The term public services refers here to services provided by government agencies and does not include services provided by nongovernmental public-sector organizations. To avoid confusion, we will henceforth use the term administrative services for services provided directly by the government. We will use the term public services broadly to include all public-sector services, government and otherwise.

The same economic damage that tax increases cause in a shrinking and aged population can occur with pension premiums. A pay-as-you-go system transfers income from working people to retirees. It shifts income from people who have liquidity to channel into savings to people who lack comparable liquidity. A pay-as-you-go pension scheme thus reduces the overall capacity for savings in Japan.

Any consideration of appropriate tax rates needs to include consideration of the premium rates for the pension program and for other social insurance. And people need to understand that any overall increase in taxation will diminish the economy in a shrinking and aged society. To repeat, we need to be wary of government claims that the aging of society requires increases in fiscal expenditures and in taxes.

FISCAL BALANCE WITHOUT TAX INCREASES

We will take a look here at what might happen to Japan's fiscal balance in the absence of tax increases. In our examination, we will consider national and local taxes together. Including local taxes is important because local governments bear a growing share of the cost of public services.

Figure 32 presents fiscal spending and tax revenues as a percentage of national income. We assume here that public works spending—excluding administrative services—will be the threshold amount: the maximum amount of spending possible without crowding out private-sector capital spending. For per capita spending on administrative services, our projections present two scenarios. One scenario is the increase in overall fiscal outlays that will result if the recent upward trend in per capita spending on administrative services continues. The other is what might result from restraint in that spending. Our figures for fiscal outlays include interest payments on national and local government bonds. The projection for tax revenues as a percentage of national income is a straight line because we assume no tax increase or decrease.

Absent restraint in per capita spending on administrative services, fiscal outlays continue upward, and the upward trend steepens around 2013. The widening gap between fiscal outlays and tax revenues is an

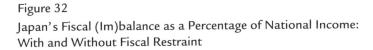

Figure 32
Japan's Fiscal (Im)balance as a Percentage of National Income:
With and Without Fiscal Restraint

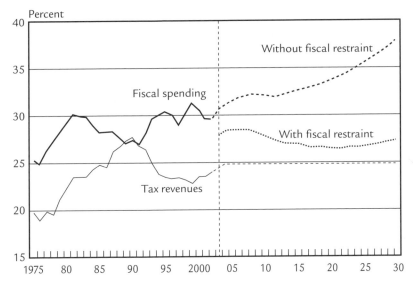

Sources: Calculations by the author on the basis of national accounts data published by
the Japanese government for the years to 2002 and projections by the author for
subsequent years

unsustainable fiscal deficit. Fiscal spending increases to 37.8% of national income in 2030, from 29.5% in 2002, and the fiscal deficit increases to 34.4% of fiscal spending, from 20.8%, over the same period.

The Japanese government does not issue long-term fiscal projections, so we don't know how much of an increase in fiscal spending it assumes in its economic forecasts. Government pronouncements, however, do not suggest much in the way of plans for curtailing fiscal spending. We must therefore conclude that the government assumptions about long-term fiscal expenditure resemble the upper curve in figure 32. And that would indeed require a tax increase.

We have seen, however, that Japanese demographics include factors that will reduce the need for fiscal spending. Equally important is the unlikelihood that spending on administrative services will continue to increase at the recent rate. That spending began increasing rapidly in the early 1990s, which coincided with an increase in the over-65 percentage of Japanese (figure 4, page 9). Despite that apparent correlation, we find a more-compelling reason for the growth in spending on administrative services: the simultaneous surge in spending on public works projects.

Numerous politicians, government agencies, and private-sector interests exercise influence in the political process of drafting a budget. Add-on provisions for increased spending on administrative services presumably received clear passage amid the spending frenzy on public works projects. Japan was trying to spend its way out of the recession that followed the collapse of its bubble economy, and we can easily surmise that administrative services were part of the general trend.

So spending on administrative services reached a presumably inflated level in the 1990s, and we have little reason to expect that spending to rise further on a per capita basis. Demographic trends will permit reduced per capita spending on some items, such as education, even as aging necessitates increased per capital spending on others. We can therefore assume that population shrinkage will reduce overall spending on administrative expenses. That assumption is the basis for the lower line for fiscal spending in figure 32.

The lower line for fiscal spending is a lot closer to the line for tax revenues. Japan's average fiscal deficit for the years from 2002 to 2030 narrows to 8.7% of fiscal spending. Reducing fiscal spending by that percentage, in other words, would eliminate the need for a tax increase. That would still require a huge effort, but the modest size of the implied deficit reveals that tax increase is less inevitable than the government suggests.

THE CASE FOR PERPETUAL PUBLIC BONDS

Restraining per capita spending on administrative services to the level of the 1990s would require substantial reductions in overall spending. The potential for achieving those reductions and an additional reduction of nearly 9% is uncertain at best. Reducing the fiscal deficit without raising taxes will demand innovative new approaches. One promising approach is the issuance of perpetual public bonds.

Payments of principal and interest on national and local government bonds account for a big part of Japan's aggregate fiscal expenditures. In 2002, those payments accounted for 16.9% of fiscal expenditures in

Japan. Issuing perpetual bonds, which yield interest in perpetuity but never mature, would eliminate the burden of principal repayments. National and local government bodies could raise funds to redeem bonds at maturity by issuing perpetual bonds. The newly issued bonds, by definition, would never require redemption.

Long-term bonds generally carry higher interest rates than short-term bonds, and that might mean somewhat higher interest costs for the bond issuers. The difference between 10-year and 20-year bonds is minimal, however, in the world's bond markets, so we can assume that the incremental cost increase would be small. A market would develop immediately for the bonds, which would enable the bondholders to liquidate their bonds at will, and that liquidity would help minimize any cost premium associated with the perpetual bonds.

Levying taxes to raise funds to redeem public bonds is, in a sense, ludicrous. The issuers of public bonds are, ultimately, the people. And the owners of the bonds, notwithstanding a relative handful of foreign investors, are mainly Japanese. So perpetual bonds eliminate the inefficiencies of recirculating funds among Japanese.

The bond issuers need to honor their obligations, of course, to their bondholders. All Japanese benefit, theoretically, from the undertakings funded with the bond proceeds, but only a minority of Japanese invest in bonds. Those investors deserve reliable interest payments and a liquid market for their bond holdings. The issuers would be fully responsible for the interest payments, and, as noted, a liquid market for the bonds would develop immediately.

No one would lose anything in the switchover to perpetual bonds. National and local governments could maintain public services without raising taxes. Bondholders would enjoy the same income and security that they have enjoyed with bonds of specified maturities.

Perpetual bonds have a well-established history in the world's capital markets. Most famous are the United Kingdom's consol bonds, first issued in the 18th century and still in circulation. Those bonds figured in the killing that Nathan Rothschild made in the London capital market after the Battle of Waterloo. His messenger brought news of the British and Prussian victory slightly before Wellington's envoy arrived. Rothschild promptly drove down prices by selling securities in a manner designed to imply that Napoleon had won the battle. After the market collapsed, he bought up securities at bargain-basement prices and emerged with huge sway over the British economy.

Historical anecdotes aside, perpetual bonds offer a serious option for coping with Japan's public-sector debt. That debt has burgeoned to ¥600 trillion, and repaying it by traditional means is utterly unrealistic. We mustn't spare Japan's policy makers the criticism they richly deserve for allowing the debt to reach that unmanageable size. But nor must we allow efforts to pay down that debt to lower living standards. Raising taxes would lower living standards, of course, and so would paring public services, since that would oblige people to pay out of their own pockets for services formerly provided by public-sector agencies. Note that bondholders would suffer along with other Japanese from a tax increase or from a diminution of public services.

Relieving the national and local governments of the burden of redeeming bonds carries the risk of encouraging renewed fiscal irresponsibility. Japan could address that risk by prohibiting the issuance of new debt beyond the original refinancing with perpetual bonds. No additional bonds should be necessary, since fiscal spending should not need to rise. Japan has the opportunity here to balance its fiscal accounts for the first time in half a century. The nation should act forthrightly on that opportunity.

FISCAL POLICY IN A SHRINKING, AGED SOCIETY

Japanese need to decide democratically how much fiscal spending is appropriate. They mustn't allow themselves, however, to fund any increase in fiscal spending through increased public debt. Increasing public debt might have made sense in an era when the economy was expanding and incomes were rising. In that era, investment by the present generation in public infrastructure supported the gains in income enjoyed by subsequent generations. Incomes will stop rising, though, in Japan's shrinking, aged society. The present generation, by living beyond its means, would lower living standards for subsequent generations. Japanese today would be forcing their children and grandchildren to foot the bill for their extravagance. In a shrinking and aged society, each generation needs to live within its means and maintain fiscal balance.

Some will argue that Japan needs to retain the option of deficit spending to cope with temporary economic downturns. Deficit spending is only a reliable economic stimulus, however, when the economy is growing over the long term. It is ineffective in stimulating the economy in a shrinking, aged society.

Fiscal measures for stimulating the economy are analogous to priming a pump: they are for kindling latent potential for capital spending and personal consumption. That pump priming only prompts corporations to undertake new investment, however, if future growth in demand is a viable possibility.

Absent convincing prospects for growth in demand, corporations will not invest in equipment that will require a decade or so to depreciate. Overall demand in Japan is destined, however, to decline steadily, as we saw in figure 12 (page 38). The principles of sound management will oblige companies to reduce, not increase, their stock of plant and equipment.

People recognize, meanwhile, that deficit spending by the government today will soon necessitate a tax increase or the equivalent, a reduction in public services. They are unlikely to increase their personal consumption in response to a fiscally induced temporary upturn in incomes.

Instilling a commitment to balanced fiscal budgets will encourage discretion in funding public services. People will recognize that spending beyond current revenues will result immediately in higher taxes. They will therefore focus fiscal expenditures on services and projects of compelling value. That will enable Japan to achieve the fiscal restraint indicated in the lower line in figure 32 (page 125). And that is the right fiscal policy for a shrinking, aged society.

CHAPTER V

A New Social Perspective on Abundance: Focusing on Quality of Life

Rising Wage Levels

THE MEANING OF NATIONAL STRENGTH

We have examined the implications of population shrinkage and aging for Japan's national economy, for its regional economies, for its public pension program, and for its public services. In the remaining chapters, we will examine more closely what the impending changes will mean for personal lifestyles. We will begin with the outlook for per capita national income, which is the chief determinant of living standards.

Analyzing economic trends from the perspective of personal lifestyles remains a novel approach in Japan. The overall size of the nation's GDP and Japan's GDP ranking in comparison with other nations retain a powerful fascination for Japanese. People are obsessed with GDP, even though it has no direct bearing on living standards in a shrinking-population economy.

That Japan has the world's second-largest GDP is a source of pride and comfort for Japanese. Japan will have the lowest economic growth rate among the industrialized nations in the years ahead, however, and uncertainty about how long Japan can cling to its "No. 2" standing is a source of concern. That concern has even prompted the government to inaugurate research on the effects of population shrinkage on national strength.

The time has come for a careful appraisal of the meaning of national strength. Constitutionally barred from possessing the means of military aggression, Japan has renounced military power as a source of national strength. That leaves the economy as a likely candidate for measuring the strength of the nation. Japan's GDP is more than three times larger than those of France and the United Kingdom. Few Japanese, however, regard their nation as three times stronger on the world stage than those two European powers.

The disparity between economic scale and people's perceptions of their nation's global clout exposes the concept of national strength as an anachronism. Speaking of national strength in terms of GDP and population might have made some sense in the 19th century. Measures of national strength have changed profoundly, however, at least since World War II.

In the industrialized world, people's expectations of their nations have focused increasingly on the standard of living. That shift in priorities should shape our concern about the implications of population shrinkage for Japan's national vitality. We should concern ourselves more with the prospects for Japan's standard of living than with the outlook for its GDP. This understanding, unfortunately, has yet to take hold in the Japanese government.

JAPAN'S LASTING ABUNDANCE

Numerous factors determine perceptions of prosperity, but per capita income is the most compelling indicator for the standard of living. Figure 33 presents trends in per capita income and in other facets of national income in Japan. The author has plotted the past and future trends for each indicator as indices of the level in 2000. Per capita income peaks in 2013, but its subsequent decline is gradual. In 2030, per capita income is only 1.2% lower than in 2000. Average personal income remains basically unchanged because the population and the GDP shrink in tandem.

Currency exchange rates and national differences in the cost of living complicate comparisons of the standard of living in different nations. But per capita income in Japan was about equal to that in the United States in 2000, and it was more than 50% higher than per capita income in Germany and in France. So we can be certain that Japan will remain among the world's most prosperous nations in 2030.

Demographic aging began in European nations before it got started in Japan, and Japanese have thus looked to Europe for insights into what

Figure 33
Japanese Per Capita National Income and Wage and Salary Levels

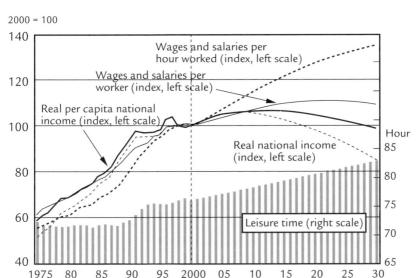

Sources: Calculations by the author on the basis of national accounts data published by
the Japanese government for the years to 2001 and projections by the author for
subsequent years

lies in store for their nation. Japan's higher per capita income, however, suggests that Japanese can achieve a more-prosperous aged society than their European counterparts. Commentators frequently cite Sweden as a successful example of engineering a high standard of living. Japan's per capita income is about 40% higher than Sweden's, which should position Japanese well to maintain social abundance amid demographic aging.

JAPAN'S POSTWAR ECONOMIC FAILURE TO IMPROVE THE QUALITY OF LIFE

Most Japanese would scoff at the suggestion that their nation ranks among the most prosperous in the world. Japan's undeniably impressive growth in GDP has not generated comparable gains in the quality of life. A big reason for that paradox is the low level of labor productivity in Japan. In the 1990s, labor productivity in Japan was only 92.3% as high as in Germany and in France. The 1990s, to be sure, were a time of economic stagnation in Japan that followed the collapse of the nation's bubble economy. But Japan's relative labor productivity was even lower in the 1980s, at 79.2% of the German and French levels.

Responsibility for Japan's poor performance in labor productivity lies with Japanese industry. Manufacturers invested excessively in automation in pursuit of increased production volumes. We examined the economic ramifications of that ill-considered investment in chapter 2.

Japanese have achieved high per capita income despite low labor productivity by working long hours and by putting a large portion of their population to work. The average Japanese workweek in the 1990s was 43.7 hours. That compares with 38.3 hours in Germany and 38.7 hours in France. More than one-half of all Japanese—53.1%—were working in the 1990s. In contrast, only 44.0% of the Germans and only 38.6% of the French held jobs. Note that the over-65 percentage of the population in the 1990s was about the same in Japan, Germany, and France (figure 1, page 3), so the higher percentage of working Japanese was no mere demographic fluke.

Wage and salary levels appear to explain why Japanese work long and in large numbers. At purchasing power parity, Germans earned the equivalent of $15.80 per hour in the 1990s, French $16.00, and Japanese only $11.70. An hour's compensation purchased only about three-fourths as much for Japanese as it did for Germans and for French.

Japanese thus lack the sense of ease that their high per capita income might suggest. Translating Japan's economic attainment into a higher quality of life will mean shortening the workweek and giving people more time to indulge in personal interests, such as hobbies, physical exercise, and even participation in social movements. Some people, of course, insist that they experience their greatest fulfillment through work. But leisure is essential to fulfilling the humanistic potential and responsibility of society. Away from the workplace, people are free to decide how to spend their time. That freedom of choice exemplifies the notion of individual liberty that has guided social progress in Western civilization.

Japan's postwar economic development thus obliged Japanese to endure low wage and salary levels and minimal leisure even as their nation built the world's second-largest GDP. Low wages and salaries are partly attributable to the low labor productivity already noted. They are also attributable to the relatively low percentage of value-added that industry has shared with employees.

We saw in figure 13 (page 44) that wage and salary gains have lagged productivity growth markedly in Japan. Japanese workers have benefited far less from their productivity gains than their counterparts in other industrialized nations. That is largely the consequence, as we have seen, of the massive and systematic suppression of wages and salaries. Japanese companies have stifled employee compensation to maximize retained earnings for reinvestment in plant and equipment.

The disproportionately large weighting of investment in the Japanese economy resulted initially from the postwar policy of promoting "detour production." That policy, as we saw in chapter 2, addressed material shortages by favoring the production of capital goods over consumer goods. The oil crises of the 1970s transformed the structure of Japanese industry, however, and we might have expected the investment weighting in Japan's economy to decline amid that transformation. That the weighting did not decline is a reflection of Japanese companies' frenetic investment in automation.

Japanese industry relentlessly pursued a strategy of maximizing sales even at the cost of minimizing return on investment. That strategy kept the population busy while denying workers the opportunity to share fully in the fruits of their labors.

PROSPERITY THROUGH POPULATION SHRINKAGE AND AGING

Overall growth in production will become impossible as Japan's population shrinks and ages, and corporate managements will need to concentrate on streamlining operations. Companies will strive to raise the value-added per unit of production as investment risk mounts and as downsizing becomes inevitable. Rising production efficiency and declining capital spending will tend to increase the percentage of production value-added that companies share with workers. Conversely, the failure of companies to raise salaries and wages would cause the Japanese economy—and demand for the companies' goods—to shrink even more than the author's projection.

The shrinking and aging of Japan's population will thus help resolve the chief flaw in the nation's economic performance: the failure to translate GDP growth into comparable gains in the standard of living. In figure 33, the thick dotted line traces the author's projection for hourly worker compensation. The projected future rise in hourly compensation is somewhat slower than the historical growth trend, but it remains robust, supported by technological advances and by workers' growing share of production value-added. Average compensation per hour is 34.8% higher in 2030 than in 2000. The author calculates that workers' share of production value-added will rise to 91.8% in 2030, from 86.5% in 2000.

Gains in hourly compensation will more than offset the shrinking workweek, and annual compensation per worker will grow, as indicated by the thin solid line in figure 33. The author projects that average annual compensation in 2030 will be 9.1% higher than in 2000. We can regard the rise in hourly compensation as enabling the decline in hours worked and a corresponding increase in leisure time. As indicated by the vertical bars in figure 33, weekly leisure time per worker increases to 82.9 hours in 2030, from 76.0 hours in 2000. Economists ordinarily include all nonworking hours, including time spent sleeping, in leisure time, but that misrepresents the category of leisure. The author has therefore subtracted eight hours per day to account for sleeping and other activity that is neither leisure nor work.

Compared with the 2.4-fold growth between 1970 and 2000, the 9.1% growth in wage and salary levels between 2000 and 2030 seems minuscule. But in combination with the projected increase in leisure time, that growth represents a significant improvement in the standard of living. And that improvement will be partly due to changes in economic structure and in corporate behavior forced by population shrinkage and aging.

The projected 9.1% increase in per capita income between 2000 and 2030 is for working Japanese. Per capita income for all Japanese will be basically unchanged over that span, but it will remain high by international standards. And the overall increase in leisure time will mean an unmistakable improvement in the standard of living. Concerns about a decline in Japan's national strength are therefore unwarranted. Japanese economic policy has impoverished the populace in terms of quality of life even while building the world's second-largest economy. All Japanese will benefit to the extent that government and industry abandon that policy.

FREEDOM NOT TO WORK—
CHANGING MODES OF EMPLOYMENT

LIFETIME EMPLOYMENT AND SENIORITY-BASED COMPENSATION

Population shrinkage and aging will occasion profound change in Japanese lifestyles. Most striking will be the end of the system of lifetime employment and seniority-based compensation that shaped the socioeconomic development of postwar Japan definitively. Numerous corporations in Japan have begun introducing elements of performance-based compensation and promotion. But far more fundamental change lies in store for Japanese employment practices.

Performance-based initiatives at Japanese corporations have thus far taken place as adjustments within the framework of lifetime employment and seniority-based compensation. To be sure, the foundations of lifetime employment might appear to be crumbling amid those initiatives and widespread corporate restructuring. The victims of restructuring, however, have been mainly older workers. Younger workers at Japanese corporations continue to enjoy the assurance of long-term employment, and their compensation continues to reflect their seniority, albeit subject to performance-based adjustments.

Trends in the mode of employment demand careful attention because of their far-reaching effects on lifestyles and corporate behavior. A social framework predicated on Japanese-style lifetime employment and seniority-based compensation differs fundamentally from one predicated on Western-style merit-based personnel policies. The uncertain fluidity of the latter is in stark contrast with the predictable stability of the former.

Japan's system of lifetime employment and seniority-based compensation is a product of the nation's wartime economic system. A government directive in 1939 linked wages to age, and a 1940 directive prohibited workers from moving from one company to another. Government officials perceived rising wages as a threat to the war effort, and they regarded worker mobility as upward pressure on wage levels.

The employment system that had served as a means of prosecuting the war became a tool for pursuing economic growth. Curtailing worker compensation remained a government priority, and the youthful weighting of the workforce meant that seniority-based compensation would minimize personnel costs for industry. Workers younger than 30 now account for only about 22% of the Japanese workforce. Statistically consistent data is unavailable for the early postwar years, but we can be certain that more than one-half of the workforce was younger than 30. Accompanying seniority-based compensation with lifetime employment made low wages palatable for young workers by assuring them of annual raises.

Another reason for retaining the wartime employment system was the desire to motivate workers and to foster employee loyalty toward companies. And the system succeeded spectacularly in regard to both of those goals. Japanese manufacturing became the marvel of the world in the 1980s on the strength of unprecedented attainment in quality control and cost reduction. People scrutinized Japanese industry for insights into the management systems presumably responsible for that attainment. Japanese attainment in quality control and cost reduction was not due, however, to any special management system. It was instead due mainly to the motivation and the company loyalty of Japanese workers.

Japanese manufacturers famously asserted international competitiveness by creating low-cost, high-quality products. That was a dramatic reversal from the "shoddy-but-cheap" approach that characterized Japanese manufacturing before the war and in the immediate postwar years. Japanese manufacturers were inferior to their North American and European counterparts in technological development capabilities. Concentrating on low-cost, high-quality production was a way to bypass that handicap. And the employee commitment and fidelity engendered by lifetime employment and seniority-based compensation were essential to that production strategy.

The hallmark of Japanese products, more than long-term durability or technological innovation, has been defect-free quality "out of the box." That quality is a tribute to the conscientious accuracy of Japanese employees in the manufacturing workplace. Japan's employment system was instrumental in attaining that world-class performance from workers at minimal cost.

IMPLICATIONS OF LIFETIME EMPLOYMENT AND SENIORITY-BASED COMPENSATION

Seniority-based compensation, as practiced in Japan, rewards employees for remaining with the same company and penalizes them for switching employers. It also encourages people to remain at their jobs continuously. Extended leaves of absence mean falling behind in seniority, and that can entail a substantial loss in cumulative income over a career.

Fealty to the company is a prerequisite for regular pay raises and promotions under Japan's lifetime employment system. Everyone at the same company tends to adopt similar values and a similar perspective. The company, meanwhile, becomes far more than a mere employer. It becomes a defining element of its employees' existence. Ask an American or European what they do for a living, and they are likely to cite their vocation: "I'm an accountant (lathe operator, mechanical engineer, etc.)." Japanese are more likely to name their company: "I work for Toyota (Toshiba, Nintendo, etc.)."

People in Japan build their lives around their company to an extent inconceivable in other industrialized nations. For Japanese employees, companies shape values and—through the long workweek and the near impossibility of extended vacations—claim an inordinate amount of time. The total immersion in company life prevents people from developing original lifestyles.

Lifetime employment and seniority-based promotions encompass corporate management, as well as the shop floor. The number of positions naturally declines toward the top of the corporate hierarchy, resulting in a pyramidal structure. That places immense pressure on companies to keep growing. Only through growth can they fulfill their promise of regular promotions and raises for all employees. That is a big reason for the obsession in Japanese corporate management with continuously expanding production. Employees share that obsession, since they recognize that corporate growth maximizes their chances for continuing promotions and raises.

Japanese industry will remain wedded to lifetime employment and to seniority-based compensation as long as its core competence centers on low-cost, high-quality manufacturing. Performance-based adjustments will remain mere inflections in the traditional employment system. A wholesale shift to performance- and merit-based compensation for employees of all ages would increase job mobility dramatically, especially among young workers. It would trigger a bidding war for the services of young labor. Wages and salaries would surge, just as Japan's wartime economic policy makers feared.

Lifetime employment and seniority-based compensation have enabled Japanese companies to underpay young workers relative to worker productivity. A freer labor market would narrow the gap between productivity and compensation. Increased job mobility would dilute company loyalty, meanwhile, and diminish employees' commitment to their work. Efficiency and accuracy in the manufacturing workplace would suffer.

Abandoning lifetime employment and seniority-based compensation would thus raise costs for Japanese companies and diminish their vaunted product quality. Until Japanese industry discovers new modes of employment that resolve those issues, it will to cling to the traditional system. The supposed innovations now on display are largely measures for trimming payrolls by culling the ranks of middle-aged and older workers.

THE COLLAPSE OF THE PYRAMID

Japan had a true population pyramid in 1950, as shown in the left half of figure 34. The number of people was largest in the youngest age bracket and declined evenly up to the highest age bracket. We have seen that maintaining lifetime employment and seniority-based compensation depends on the continuing expansion of companies' workforces. Japan's population pyramid furnished exactly the kind of annual growth in young labor required to adopt that system widely.

The recent age structure of Japan's population, shown in the right half of figure 34, is utterly unsuited to lifetime employment and seniority-based compensation. Other industrialized nations already had age structures like this in the immediate postwar years. That says a lot about why lifetime employment and seniority-based compensation did not become common outside Japan.

In theory, companies could maintain lifetime employment even in the absence of an expanding workforce. They could do that by promoting people on the basis of performance and by minimizing the seniority-based component of wages and salaries. In practice, that would weaken the basis of lifetime employment. Performance-based compensation would

Figure 34
Change in Japan's Demographic Age Profile

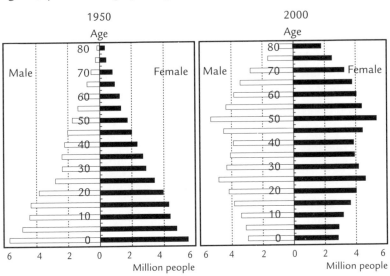

Source: Census data published by the Japanese government

encourage workers to offer their services to the highest bidder. Loyalty to employers would decline. Companies would no longer be able to get away with underpaying young workers.

Japan's population pyramid was already beginning to collapse by the early 1970s. Most first-time entrants into the full-time labor market are in the 20-to-24 age bracket, and the number of Japanese in that bracket began declining in 1971. What has permitted the broad continuation of lifetime employment and seniority-based compensation has been the growing number of working women.

The percentage of working women in the 20-to-24 age bracket turned upward in 1975 after a period of decline. More striking, however, is the surge in the percentage of working women aged 40 to 54 that began in 1976 (figure 15, page 52). Most of those women held low-wage, low-ranking jobs. That helped Japanese industry maintain a pyramidal work-force even as Japan's population lost its pyramidal structure.

Growth in the percentage of working women of all ages thus filled the population trough between the first and second baby booms. Japan's second-generation baby boomers—the second peak in the nation's demographic profile—entered the 20-to-24 age range in 1982. Growth in the percentage of working women is slowing, however, and the number of Japanese aged 20 to 24 resumed shrinking in 1995.

Japanese industry will soon become unable to maintain even the semblance of a pyramidal workforce. The end is near for Japan's traditional system of lifetime employment and seniority-based compensation.

COMPENSATION BASED ON VALUE-ADDED

Figure 35 presents wage-and-salary levels by age bracket in Japan, France, Germany, and the United Kingdom. (Comparable data is unavailable for the United States.) Note that Japan's compensation curve shows a sharper inclination than the other nations'.

As noted, young workers in Japan accept low pay in return for the promise of lifetime employment and steadily rising compensation. Statistically consistent data is unavailable for absolute wage and salary levels in the different nations, so we cannot be certain exactly how much lower young workers' compensation is in Japan than in the other nations. But the available data suggests that wages and salaries for young people are substantially lower in Japan.

Lifetime employment and seniority-based compensation are uncommon in France, Germany, and the United Kingdom. So we can assume that Japan's compensation curve will resemble theirs after the collapse of the traditional Japanese employment system. This does not mean, however, that a flatter compensation curve will mean an across-the-board rise in compensation for young workers. Nor does it mean that compensation for all middle-aged and older workers will cease rising or even decline.

Although the curves in figure 35 are averages for each age bracket, the curve for Japan applies to nearly all workers. Japanese wages and salaries in each age bracket cluster in a narrow band. Compensation varies somewhat, of course, among companies and among industries. But the disparity is remarkably small. Companies that offered compensation substantially lower than the norm would be unable to attract employees, and employers have had little incentive to offer compensation substantially higher than the norm.

Big change is in store. The end of seniority-based compensation will oblige companies to pay employees on the basis of their individual

Figure 35
An International Comparison of Wage and Salary Differentials by Age

Level for workers aged 20 to 24 = 100

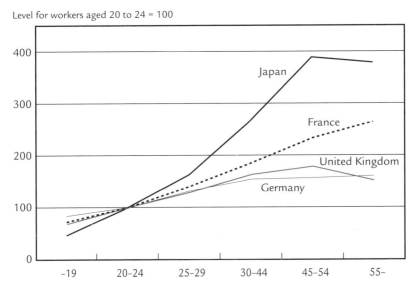

Sources: Comparative international labor data published by the Japan Institute for Labor
Policy and Training (male workers in manufacturing industries; 1997 data for
Japan, 1995 data for the other nations)

contribution to value-added. Figure 36 presents a model of a possible result of that change. The thick line is the same curve that represented an index of Japanese compensation in figure 35. But in figure 36, the vertical axis indicates actual compensation.

Workers who generate little value-added will receive lower-than-average compensation. Even in the 20-to-24 age bracket, compensation could well decline for some workers. And those workers will continue to receive lower-than-average pay if their value-added remains lower than average. Their compensation curve appears in figure 36 as curve A. Curve B in the figure indicates the high compensation that workers who generate higher-than-average value-added will earn. And curve C indicates the average compensation for Japanese workers in the post-lifetime employment era.

Figure 36
Japan's Impending Stratification of Wage and Salary Differentials by Age

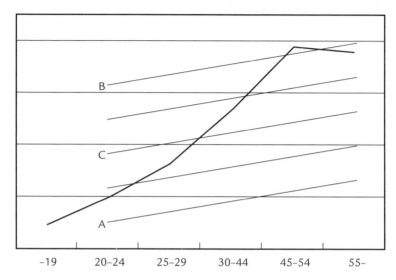

Source: Labor data published by the Japan Institute for Labor Policy and Training
(male workers in manufacturing industries, 1997) for the aggregate curve

SPECIALTY-BASED COMPENSATION

Hourly value-added per worker varies by job category, and future compensation in Japan will reflect that variance. In seniority-based compensation, wages and salaries have reflected the average value-added of all workers of the same age at each company. In value-added–based compensation, materials handlers, assembly line workers, warehouse managers, shipping clerks, salespeople, and employees in other job categories will all receive different compensation.

The "ability" in the ability-based compensation that will succeed seniority-based compensation comprises two elements: the basic ability to qualify for a job category and the ability to excel in that work. We can characterize the former ability as a specialty and the latter as a skill. Compensation will differ more among specialties than among skill levels in each specialty. Automated manufacturing, for example, minimizes the productivity differentials among workers in the same job category.

In figure 36, the range of compensation curves basically reflects the compensation disparities among specialties. Compensation curves for different skill levels will cluster around the curves for different specialties. Employees' rising skill levels account for the upward incline of the compensation curves. Workers who attain skills that qualify them for higher-value-added specialties will be able to jump to higher compensation curves.

Overall wage-and-salary levels will depend somewhat on trends in labor productivity and on the balance of power between labor and management. Wages and salaries for young workers appear certain to rise, however, in the wake of the collapse of seniority-based compensation. The new employment system will tend to raise young workers' compensation into convergence with their value-added. Tightening supply and demand will also tend to raise compensation for young workers as the number of young people in Japan declines.

The picture is more complex in regard to middle-aged and older workers. Properly, compensation for those workers should rise. Industry, as we have seen, shares a smaller percentage of value-added with workers in Japan than in other nations. And the declining need for capital spending will leave Japanese industry with increased leeway to raise wages and salaries. The message that emerges from Japanese management, however, suggests that companies will seek to lower compensation for middle-aged and older workers. That will encounter inevitable resistance from employees who accepted low pay while young in the expectation of higher compensation later. Compensation for middle-aged and older workers will thus be subject to multiple and counteracting variables, but let us assume tentatively that it will decline somewhat.

THE COLLAPSE OF LIFETIME EMPLOYMENT

The changing age structure of Japan's population needn't, in itself, force an end to lifetime employment. Companies could maintain lifetime employment, as we have seen, by abandoning seniority-based compensation and promotions. Rather, what will put an end to lifetime employment will be the need for streamlining, as outlined in chapter 2.

Streamlining companies will mean revamping product portfolios and production processes, as well as downsizing operations. The changing composition of demand will call for dropping some products and adding others. Some manufacturers will opt to purchase semifinished goods from suppliers. That will enable them to shut down front-end materials processing and thereby reduce their stocks of production equipment and shrink their workforces.

Lifetime employment would hinder companies in accomplishing the transformation necessitated by Japan's shrinking and aging population. Companies will require the freedom to dismiss employees engaged in discontinued operations and to hire new employees who possess the specialties needed for new products and operations. Numerous Japanese companies have attempted in recent years to switch over to new lines of business, but few have succeeded, partly because of their adherence to lifetime employment and the resultant mismatch between human resources and specialties. Employees who only yesterday were working on an assembly line are unlikely to be reborn today as stellar salespersons.

Labor also stands to benefit from the end of lifetime employment. Offsetting the undeniable appeal of stable employment are the fading prospects of annual advances in compensation and in rank. Achieving those advances will depend increasingly on mastering new specialties. When employers do not require employees' newly acquired specialties or do not value them sufficiently, the employees will earn more by moving to other companies. The end of seniority-based compensation will facilitate that movement by eliminating the traditional penalty associated with the loss of seniority.

Eliminating the penalty for changing employers is especially noteworthy. That penalty has persuaded numerous Japanese over the years to remain at companies where they felt uncomfortable and to remain in jobs that they found unsatisfactory. True labor mobility will give employees, along with management, an interest in abandoning lifetime employment. That could mean a surprisingly swift demise for the most distinctively Japanese of Japan's employment traditions.

WORKERS' ULTIMATE FREEDOM

Elements of lifetime employment could survive the collapse of Japan's traditional employment system. The principle of forging an enduring covenant between employers and employees has vigorous proponents in Japan and in other industrialized nations. Numerous large corporations in North America and in Europe observe some kind of lifetime employment. Any future application of lifetime employment in Japan will differ fundamentally, however, from the traditional practice: it will honor workers' freedom to change employers.

Lifetime employment and seniority-based compensation, as practiced in Japan, have robbed workers of the freedom to change employers. The Japanese system has, in effect, chained workers to their companies. It has locked employees into the value systems of their companies and usurped their time. Freedom to change jobs will do more, however, than simply loosen the ties that have bound workers to their employers. It will enable them to work when and only as much as they choose.

In the absence of substantial penalties for changing jobs, increasing numbers of people will stop working altogether for extended periods. They will work just long enough to save money to embark on the adventure or vacation or other personal project of their dreams. Japan's ranks of generally young "freeters" include numerous individuals who have adopted that approach. Freeter is an amalgamation of "free arbeiter." The Japanese have adopted the German word for work, arbeit, in reference to part-time or short-term jobs.

Japan's employment system has placed freeters at a disadvantage and has thereby limited the number of people who have opted for that lifestyle. Choosing the freeter option will become commonplace, however, as Japanese gain the previously unimaginable freedom not to work.

The history of modernization is a tale of liberating people from work. Technological progress has reduced the number of hours that people need to work daily to earn their sustenance. The freedom not to work—the freedom to work when and as the individual chooses—is a natural result of that historical trend. It will transform life in Japan just as profoundly as did the industrialization policies adopted after the Meiji Restoration of 1868 and the labor policies adopted after World War II. An unprecedented diversity of lifestyles will emerge.

Possessing a vocational specialty will be a prerequisite for enjoying the new freedom fully. Wages and salaries will henceforth vary greatly depending on whether workers possess or do not possess specialties and on what kinds of specialties they possess. Freeters who have acquired high-earning specialties will enjoy immense freedom. Those who have not will need to accept wages at the bottom end of a broadening disparity of compensation.

DIVERSIFYING LIFESTYLES IN
A DISPERSING POPULATION

The shrinking and aging of Japan's population change a crucial condition in population distribution. Our projections for population distribution in chapter 3 included the assumption that recent trends in population movement among prefectures would continue. We saw that the populations of Japan's largest metropolitan areas are destined to age greatly. The youthful components of those populations will shrink sharply even if inflows of people continue at their recent rate. Those inflows are likely to slow, however, on account of structural change in Japan's economy wrought by population shrinkage and aging.

Regional differentials in wage and salary levels are bound to narrow, as we saw in chapter 3, and that will reduce the motivation for people to move to the large metropolitan areas. Here, we will examine some other reasons to expect substantial change in the patterns of population movement. We will see that changes in the conditions for population distribution, combined with changes in modes of employment, will stimulate increasing diversity in lifestyles.

VOTING WITH THEIR FEET

The American political economist C. M. Tiebout famously observed that people vote with their feet in regard to regional public services. That is, people express their preferences in regard to public policy at the ballot box, but they express their valuation of the resultant public services through their choice of where to live. That valuation reflects judgments about the value of public services received relative to the tax burden borne.

In Japan, little movement of population has occurred as a result of people voting with their feet in regard to taxes and public services. Japan has a highly federalized system of government, and public services and tax rates are essentially identical everywhere in the nation. That uniformity will change, however, as a result of the ongoing devolution of power from the central government to the 47 prefectural governments. The ultimate extent of that devolution remains unclear, but we know that prefectural governments will end up administering numerous public services presently administered by the central government. And we know that they will need to fund a big part of those services with locally generated tax revenue. Those developments are certain to spawn diversity in public services among prefectures. They could also spawn regional disparity in tax rates. That would set the stage for Japanese to begin voting with their feet.

We can infer a lot about likely future trends in population movement from the regional economic projections presented in chapter 3. Let us assume that any devolution of taxation authority will provide initially for maintaining public services at their present level. That will mean compensating for regional disparity in tax revenue through subsidies and revenue sharing. Disparity, of course, is inevitable. For example, the vast majority of Japan's large corporations maintain their headquarters in Japan's metropolitan areas—mainly in Tokyo. Taxing corporations at their headquarters domicile would route the bulk of corporate tax receipts to the metropolitan prefectures.

Maintaining regional uniformity through subsidies and revenue sharing managed by the central government is antithetical, however, to the principle of devolution. Japan's prefectural governments will eventually need to shoulder more responsibility for managing their fiscal accounts and for coordinating industrial and economic activity in their domains.

We are assuming that the prefectures will maintain public services initially at the present level, so per capita spending on public services will be approximately the same nationwide. On the other side of the fiscal equation, per capita tax revenue will reflect trends in income levels (figure 28, page 99). Prefectures where per capita tax revenue increases will enjoy an improvement in their fiscal position, and those where per capita tax revenue decreases will suffer a worsening of their fiscal position. Thus, figure 28's projected changes in income levels are equivalent to changes in the fiscal condition of regional governments.

We saw in chapter 4 that Japan should not need to raise taxes to keep its fiscal accounts in balance while maintaining public services at their 1990's level. That is our conclusion, however, for the nation overall. At the regional level, tax increases will become necessary in some prefectures, whereas tax cuts will become possible in others.

Figure 28 reveals that the fiscal position of prefectural governments will worsen in Japan's three largest metropolitan areas and in some of their surrounding prefectures. Fiscal conditions will worsen most in the Tokyo region, followed by the Hanshin region (centered on Osaka); the Chukyo region (centered on Nagoya); and Ibaraki and Tochigi prefectures (both near Tokyo). Per capita income is certain to decline in all of those regions and prefectures, even if population inflows continue. Prefectural government finances are also likely to come under pressure in the prefectures of Nara, Shizuoka, Kyoto, Hokkaido, Hiroshima, and Gunma. Our projections for per capita income in those prefectures show increases when we assume no population movement, but they show declines when we assume continued population movement—outflows in regard to these prefectures—at the recent rates.

Prefectural governments in the above regions and prefectures will presumably need to raise taxes to maintain public services at the present level. And the tax hikes will need to be even bigger than we might surmise from figure 28. That is because those regions and prefectures are unprepared to accommodate aged populations. Their unpreparedness is understandable, since their populations remain relatively young. But they are all about to experience rapid aging, and that will impose new burdens on public services.

Governments of prefectures where per capita income rises will, conversely, enjoy the luxury of lowering taxes. However, a caveat: Underlying the projections presented in figure 28 is the assumption that industry will allocate capital in ways that employ labor maximally. The assumption, in other words, is that investment will adapt optimally to the changing geographic distribution of labor. That will depend partly on prefectural government policies. So tax cuts will not necessarily become possible in all of the prefectures where figure 28 indicates rises in per capita income. But they are a real possibility, especially where our projections indicate rises in per capita income regardless of trends in population movement.

Those prefectures also enjoy another fiscal advantage. The over-65 percentage of their populations is high, so they have already invested extensively in facilities for accommodating aged populations. That will minimize the future fiscal burden associated with aging.

Geographic disparity in taxation will change a fundamental condition in people's lifestyle choices. It will affect personal and corporate decisions about where to live and operate. People and corporations will presumably vote with their feet by eschewing high-tax prefectures in favor of more-amenable tax environments. Increasingly, they will abandon Japan's highly urbanized prefectures and head for the countryside. The narrowing of geographic differentials in wage and salary levels will reinforce that trend, as will the changing structure of Japanese industry. As we have seen, the shift in focus to consumer goods, from capital goods, will occasion smaller factories and allow industry to follow population shifts.

We cannot predict reliably how much the changing fiscal circumstances of Japan's prefectures will affect overall population movement. The nation's big cities, for example, will continue to exert compelling appeal, even as high-tax environments. We can be certain, however, that lifestyles will become more diverse. Since World War II, Japanese have gravitated to the nation's largest metropolitan areas. The urban population adopted highly uniform values, and the concentration of economic, political, and media power in the metropolitan regions served to impose those values on the entire nation.

Now, the redistribution of population and resources will occasion new values and new lifestyles. A healthy interplay of values will arise. Values rooted in the countryside will begin to influence Japan's urbanites, just as urban values long dominated the countryside. An unprecedented social vibrancy will be the result.

CITY HOMES—METROPOLITAN OR OTHERWISE—FOR THE ELDERLY

The places most likely to host growing concentrations of Japan's elderly are the urban centers of the nation's metropolitan areas and its regional cities. Growing numbers of middle-aged Japanese voice hopes of spending their retirement quietly in the countryside. That might be feasible for those who have relatives at their preferred retirement destinations. But it will prove impractical for most who do not. They will encounter a dearth of support for geriatric lifestyles outside the city.

Japan's nonurban prefectures have a head start in demographic aging, and they have, as we have seen, developed facilities and services to accommodate aged populations. Residents in their outlying districts are unlikely, though, to invest eagerly in additional infrastructure to support elderly influxes of population.

Retirees, however, will be part of the movement away from Japan's metropolitan areas. Declining per capita income in those areas will oblige local governments to resort to some combination of reduced public services and increased taxes. That could prompt some urban retirees to relocate to regional cities. Residents of those cities might well feel that the metropolises had robbed them of productive youth and spewed back unproductive old people. But they will have little choice but to accept the results of unfettered population mobility.

We should note (1) the danger that financially strapped prefectural governments might adopt policies intentionally unfriendly to elderly residents and (2) the need for the national government to ensure a minimum level of elderly support in every prefecture. The temptation to skimp on public services for the elderly will be great. Prefectures where per capita income declines could easily succumb to a fiscal vicious circle: raise taxes to maintain public services; suffer an exodus of productive, working-age residents driven away by high taxes; raise taxes further to compensate for the deteriorating tax base. This is the dark side of devolution. Japan needs to ensure that devolving authority to the prefectures does not spawn unacceptably large differentials in public services. The national government needs to continue to participate in framing policy for public services, at least in regard to the elderly.

In any case, all of Japan's prefectures will need to raise efficiency in providing public services for elderly residents. Elderly populations will burgeon in the metropolitan areas, and the over-65 percentage of the population in nonurban prefectures could rise even more than recent trends suggest. One way to raise efficiency would be to pursue economies of scale by consolidating facilities. Public service providers in metropolitan areas could integrate their core service offerings at large facilities in the city centers and subcenters. Their counterparts in Japan's outlying prefectures could integrate services at facilities in regional cities.

No or only minimal services for the elderly would be available in the suburbs of large cities and outside cities in the countryside. That might sound cruel and even undemocratic, but caring for over-65 Japanese when they account for more than 30% of the population will be a stupendous task. Bold measures will be necessary to cope with the challenge.

The ongoing transition from extended families to nuclear families will oblige elderly citizens to favor proximity to public services. Whether or not Japan takes the steps described above, services are bound to be more plentiful in urban centers than in suburbs and more plentiful in regional cities than in the country. We can therefore expect to see older Japanese gravitate to places where services are available.

A CONTINUING CONCENTRATION TOWARD THE CITIES

We have seen that Japan's long-continuing population shift toward the nation's largest metropolitan areas will end and that people will disperse outward to nonurban prefectures. The destinations for most of those people, however, will be regional cities, not isolated hillsides. In other words, Japan's population will continue to coalesce in cities, albeit a greater number and a broader geographical range of cities. The ongoing depopulation of the rural countryside will proceed unabated.

Japan's regional cities will display increasing economic and social vigor. The consolidation of regional public services in those cities will generate jobs, as will the inflow of related private-sector service providers. Other private-sector employers, such as manufacturers, will come, too, attracted by the growing populations of working-age residents.

Here again, the sharing of benefits will be unequal. The population will decline so much in some parts of Japan that cities there will be unable to grow. Those cities will fail to attain the critical mass of population and other resources necessary to develop as regional hubs. They will lose population to more-successful cities in neighboring regions and will gradually wither away. Reinforcing that trend will be the growing tendency of elderly Japanese to locate where public services are most readily available.

This is not to say, however, that rural villages will disappear from the Japanese map. Although the number of villages will dwindle, village life will remain the lifestyle choice for numerous Japanese. Pastoral settings exert powerful appeal for the growing numbers of Japanese who are interested in living closer to nature. Dramatic productivity gains in agriculture are restoring the viability of farming as a means of making a living. The combination of farming and related industries could reinvigorate the Japanese countryside. Fulfilling that potential will depend on satisfying important conditions, however, such as ensuring quality education for children. We will examine possible scenarios in chapter 6.

CHAPTER VI

A Guide Map for the Shrinking-Population Economy

OVERHAULING JAPAN'S ECONOMIC SYSTEM

Economic policy and business management in Japan need to address a simple and overriding reality: The shrinking and aging of Japan's population are inevitable, and economic shrinkage is therefore unavoidable. Stopgap measures, such as importing foreign labor, will simply delay the inevitable and shift the economic burden of coping with demographic change to later generations.

Japanese business can remain profitable, however, if managements act responsibly. Industry needs to reduce production capacity systematically in accordance with realistic projections for demand. Companies need to increase the value-added portion of sales. Managements need to resist the temptation to compensate for the declining supply of labor by investing excessively in automation. That investment, as we have seen, reduces the value-added share of sales and aggravates economic shrinkage. In addition, companies need to share their value-added with workers by at least maintaining wages and salaries at the present levels.

Economic planners and business managers need to recognize Japan's ongoing transformation to a consumption-led economy, from the investment-led economy that had prevailed since World War II. Companies need to come to terms, meanwhile, with the implications of the impending collapse of the system of lifetime employment and seniority-based compensation.

The demographic change under way in Japan thus mandates fundamental change in economic policy and in business management. In this concluding chapter, we will examine the kinds of change that will be necessary.

JAPAN'S OUTMODED FINANCIAL SYSTEM

Japanese business management has focused narrowly on sales and production volume. Executives at Japanese companies discuss their business performance largely in terms of sales growth. Comments about profitability enter the conversation, if at all, as secondary considerations. Some executives even assert that their companies can keep going on sales momentum alone. They insist that they can get by somehow, even with minimal or even negative profit margins, as long as their products are selling. Reinforcing the obsession with sales are the mass media. Sales are the primary criterion for the frequently published and carefully watched rankings of corporations in different industries. Rankings by profitability receive far less emphasis and attention.

The emphasis on sales over profitability, more than any other factor, distinguishes Japanese business management from its North American and European counterparts. Especially telling is Japanese managers' faith "that they can get by somehow, even with minimal or even negative profit margins, as long as their products are selling."

At first glance, that faith appears utterly inconsistent with the basic tenets of economics. Companies are supposed to go bankrupt if they become chronically unprofitable. Capital is supposed to abandon low-profitability enterprises in favor of more-profitable companies and more-profitable industries. Companies that thus become unable to attract capital are supposed to go bankrupt.

What has enabled Japanese business to violate the fundamental precepts of economics has been Japan's financial system. Japanese companies traditionally have secured the vast majority of their external funding from financial intermediaries, rather than directly from the marketplace. They have raised funds mainly by borrowing from banks and other financial institutions rather than by issuing stocks and bonds. Even when companies have turned to the capital market for funding, financial institutions have been important purchasers of their bond and equity issues.

Companies have built close, long-term relationships with their "main banks." Those banks have stood by their corporate customers through thick and thin, and they have been loath to call in loans even when the borrowers have become conspicuously unviable. To be sure, the relationships between corporations and banks in Japan have shown signs of change in recent years. But the basic pattern of companies relying heavily on close relationships with their main banks remains very much intact.

Corporations in North America and Europe, which rely mainly on the capital markets for their external financing, can ill afford persistently weak profitability. Disappointing dividends or concerns about a company's prospects would prompt investors to dump its stock and invest in more-promising ventures. Investors—whether institutions or individuals—have no sentimental attachment to the investee companies. Their interest centers coldly on dividends and capital gains.

Japanese corporations are unprofitable by international standards, and excessive investment in automation has been a cause of that unprofitability. What has enabled companies to persist in that investment has been the funding readily available from banks. Japanese banks, though, are approaching the limits of their capacity for funding unprofitable capital spending.

Imprudent lending has been at least partly responsible for the series of Japanese bank failures in recent years. The government has sought to shore up the traditional function of banks in funding Japanese industry. It has infused banks with public money in an effort to maintain and even expand the availability of bank financing for industry. That effort, however, is about to encounter the cold reality of shrinking-population economics.

A shrinking labor pool and shrinking demand will oblige managements to abandon the strategy of maximizing sales while accepting minimal profit margins. Corporate survival will depend on maximizing the value-added percentage of sales. Establishing and attaining suitable goals for raising that percentage are essential to reducing production capacity as Japan's shrinking population demands.

We saw in chapter 2 that the value-added percentage of sales is highest when capital intensiveness is optimal; that is, when industry deploys the amount of equipment that supports the greatest production output at the lowest overall cost. The value-added percentage of sales thus indicates how well industry is matching production capacity to the size of the workforce.

A financial system centered on bank lending fails to encourage the kind of management required in a shrinking-population economy. Japan's financial system has actually discouraged companies from striving to raise the value-added portion of sales. It has encouraged excessive capital spending. Banks have a vested interest in industrial expansion—in growing loan portfolios and in growing pools of deposits. Growth in production capacity and in sales means growth in demand for loan financing.

Well-managed companies that optimize their capital spending and maximize their value-added present less demand for loans. Another problem for banks is that well-managed, financially sound companies have good credit ratings and thus secure low interest rates, which are unprofitable for lenders.

Equity financing, unlike bank financing, encourages industry to maximize the value-added component of sales. Companies attract investors and secure reliable access to external funding by raising their value-added and by using that value-added to pay high dividends or to increase their potential for paying high dividends in the future.

A FINANCIAL SYSTEM FOCUSED ON PROFITABILITY

Reforming the financial sector needs to be the top priority in preparing Japan's economy to accommodate a shrinking population. Japan needs to shift to a financial system centered on equity financing—a system that values and rewards companies on the basis of their profitability. Encouraging industry to concentrate on maximizing profitability, rather than on maximizing production capacity and sales, will maximize living standards.

Channeling funds into low-return investments would amplify the decline in national income and lower living standards. Japan needs to maximize return on what will become a shrinking pool of savings. And a financial system centered on the stock market is the best framework for ensuring maximal return.

Equity financing will help cope with the increased risk that capital spending will entail in the shrinking-population economy. A company's access to equity funding increases or decreases continually in accordance with how well it uses that funding. Bank financing, in contrast, carries the same annual interest expense regardless of how well the borrower uses the funding. That dulls management's sensitivity to the risk associated with different investment options.

Japan's government is making a big mistake in adhering to a policy of supporting the maintenance and expansion of bank financing. The public funds that the government has poured into the banking sector are the people's hard-earned savings. Using those funds so wastefully is inexcusable, especially considering the impending and unavoidable shrinkage in the pool of national savings.

Proponents of government support for the banking sector insist that the alternative is a sharp decline in bank lending and a resultant wave of bankruptcies and unemployment. Capital tends to flow, however, toward investment opportunities where it can do the most good. Fostering a vigorous stock market will help allocate Japan's savings in ways that are maximally beneficial for the nation. Reengineering Japan's financial system to maximize return on the people's savings should be the government's chief concern in financial policy.

The stock market will need to operate freely to fulfill its potential for maximizing return on Japan's savings. Capital will need to be able to flow freely to equities that offer the highest dividends, the best prospects for capital gains, or both. A vigorous mutual funds industry will be indispensable. Asset managers at those funds have better access than most individual investors do to information about prospective investments, and they can generally do a better job of allocating assets in accordance with prescribed investment criteria. Also indispensable will be a comprehensive system for evaluating the performance of the mutual funds. Individual investors will require thorough information about the investment approaches and results of the different mutual funds.

A stock market has long existed in Japan, but it has been a market in name only. Impeding the development of the stock market has been the absence of a modern and vigorous mutual funds industry, and that absence is attributable to government financial policy that has favored the banking sector. The government has begun moving to foster a more-functional stock market by promoting the development of the mutual funds industry. Its measures have included improving the tax treatment for investments in mutual funds. But the government adheres stubbornly to a bank-centric stance even in its measures to stimulate growth in the stock market.

The government's refusal to countenance the shrinkage of the banking industry and of loan financing continues to obstruct the development of the stock market. Measures for promoting the growth of the stock market by working through the banking sector are doomed to failure. Growth in the stock market will inevitably reduce corporate demand for bank loans. The banking industry is hardly likely to cooperate actively in carrying out financial measures that will diminish its bread-and-butter business. Creating a fully functional stock market in Japan will require the government to accept a smaller banking sector and a reduction in loan financing.

We can only rue the ill-conceived financial deregulation undertaken in the 1990s under the guise of a Japanese Big Bang. The author warned at the time that consolidation in Japan's financial sector would simply reinforce banks' dominance in that sector, and that is exactly what has happened. Japan revised its antitrust legislation to permit financial holding companies, and nearly all the securities firms in the nation are now under bank control. The transition to a financial system centered on a freely functioning stock market has thus become all the more difficult. That transition will be absolutely unavoidable, however, in Japan's shrinking-population economy.

The financial system exerts tremendous influence on the national economy and on corporate management in Japan as in other nations. Yet for all its influence, the financial sector is inherently fragile, based as it is on trust. Financial panics of the past weigh heavily on the minds of financial policy makers. Those policy makers need to recognize the needs and circumstances of the present, however, and to act appropriately. They need to begin by paring Japan's unhealthy dependence on loan financing.

RESTRUCTURING THE SYSTEM OF TECHNOLOGICAL DEVELOPMENT

Population shrinkage will oblige Japan's companies to improve their capabilities in technological development. Some Japanese companies have developed internationally competitive strengths in product development, most notably in automobiles and in consumer electronics. But U.S. and European companies maintain a technological edge over their Japanese counterparts in most sectors. That edge is especially apparent, for example, n genetic engineering and in software development, two defining sectors of 21st-century industry.

Japanese business strategy has continued to center on building economies of scale. The shrinking and aging of the Japanese workforce, however, will render that strategy ineffective and will diminish the international competitiveness of Japanese companies that adhere to the traditional business model. Strengthening capabilities in technological development is an absolute condition for ensuring Japan's economic viability.

Some observers have cited differences in educational systems as the reason for the U.S. and European edge over Japan in science and technology. The author, however, believes that the reason lies elsewhere. Japanese scientists and engineers are every bit the equals of their American and European counterparts in basic competence and even in creative insight. The comparative weakness of Japanese industry in technological development is a reflection, rather, of using human resources inefficiently. That inefficiency stems from three main problems: a lack of openness in basic research and in applied research, an overly comprehensive approach to science and technology, and overly self-contained research and development programs at individual companies.

OPENNESS

The United States is the world leader in science and technology, and U.S. research and development benefit incalculably from the contributions of an international cast of scientists and engineers. Chinese and Indians have been especially prominent in the vanguard of U.S. science and technology. Japanese companies, in contrast, continue to rely almost exclusively on Japanese personnel in research and development programs. They can hardly expect to compete with U.S. and European companies that tap the best and brightest minds from around the world.

A reliance on homegrown talent prevails throughout Japanese society. That Japan has built an advanced civilization despite that insularity is a tribute to its native capabilities. But the supply of brilliant minds is a finite resource in any nation. If Japanese industry is to assert world-class strengths in technological development, it needs to start by building research and development programs that are open to the world.

Talented researchers and engineers from China and India are bypassing Japan and flocking to the United States. That is not because lucrative compensation packages await them there. On the contrary, most of them accept low salaries and endure job insecurity. What attracts scientific and engineering talent to the United States is the lure of opportunity. The opportunities are not even necessarily fair. Foreign researchers commonly receive less credit and compensation for their contributions than they deserve. But the opportunities are nonetheless real and compelling.

Scientific and engineering work in the United States is far more open than in Japan. The United States offers ready access to a huge concentration of scientific and technical information and a large and eager audience for announcements of research findings. It is rich in opportunities for commercializing those findings.

Japanese research and development would benefit immensely if Japan could attract even some of the talent that is converging on the United States. Luring scientific and engineering talent will require corporations and universities to revamp their R&D organizations and their employment systems. The increased openness of Japanese R&D and the accompanying influx of foreign talent will mean heightened competition for Japanese scientists and engineers. That will occasion renewed vitality in R&D, which will contribute toward invigorating the Japanese economy.

Focus

The second reason for the inefficient use of human resources in R&D programs is that those programs are hopelessly overextended. Japanese corporations and universities are tackling essentially every field of R&D that exists on earth. In no other nation is the scope of R&D so comprehensive. Even in the United States, some fields of research receive little or no attention. Japan has a large population and a large economy, but it cannot possibly deploy enough talent or enough funding to achieve world-class R&D in every field. Raising Japan's international profile in science and technology will depend on focusing resources more narrowly.

We need to distinguish carefully, however, between "focusing" and "prioritizing." Government policy makers use the term prioritizing frequently in reference to promoting technological development. What they are talking about is a matter of merely tweaking the allocation of resources.

They will allocate more resources to some fields of R&D than to others, but their inherent assumption is that all fields will continue to receive at least some resources. The idea is that scientists and researchers in every field will receive enough support to survive and to carry on some amount of R&D work. But the limited funding essentially precludes any hope of achieving world-class results.

True focus, on the other hand, would mean ceasing R&D in some fields completely to support genuinely world-class R&D in others. Japan's inability to achieve that kind of focus has resulted more from its industrial structure than from technological strategy. Unlike any other nation, Japan remains host to nearly every kind of industry under the sun.

Other nations focus on some industries to the exclusion of others in accordance with the principle of comparative advantage. Their work in technological development naturally tends to reflect that focus, and concentrating human resources and funding on selected fields of R&D maximizes the potential for achieving world-class results in those fields.

Success in strengthening technological development in Japan will hinge on focusing the industrial structure. Retain some industries, that is, and abandon others. This is hardly a revolutionary concept. Most nations, as a matter of common sense, concentrate on industries of comparative advantage and rely on imports for products of other industries. That is what the idea of an international division of labor is all about.

Promoting specialization—participating actively in the international division of labor—is highly desirable from the standpoint of raising productivity. Japan compares poorly with other industrialized nations in the production efficiency of industry overall. That is at least partly because Japan continues to support several industries that do not offer a comparative advantage of any kind.

Decisions about which industries to retain and which ones to abandon should not be up to government policy makers. Rather, they should arise from the workings of a free market. Eliminating tariff and nontariff barriers to imports will force Japan to focus on its industries of comparative advantage and to withdraw from industries of comparative disadvantage.

Even some supporters of this approach will call for government protection for "infant industries." They are concerned about industries that (1) do not presently offer a comparative advantage but (2) will be important to Japan's future industrial and economic development and (3) given the chance to grow promise to assert a comparative advantage in the future. Selecting which "future growth industries" to protect is problematic, however, and we should not place undue faith in the government's ability to make the right choices.

Japan's government caused serious problems for the nation by extending protective support to selected industries after World War II. That policy raised domestic prices unnecessarily. And most of the selected industries—notably steel, shipbuilding, chemicals, and oil refining—became overly large. In contrast, Japanese manufacturers received almost no government protection in consumer electronics, wristwatches, cameras, and communications equipment, among other industries. Manufacturers in those industries relied on their own resourcefulness in building successful enterprises and in becoming important exporters.

Participating actively in the international division of labor is thus desirable from the standpoint of living standards. Local industries that assert a comparative advantage will furnish high-quality products at low cost. Likewise, importing products from nations that assert a comparative advantage in those products will ensure maximal quality at minimal cost. The international division of labor thereby helps nations derive the highest-possible standards of living from their income levels. And that will be crucially important in Japan as per capita income ceases to rise.

In conclusion, specialization is absolutely essential in maximizing competitiveness in technological development. No nation can support world-class R&D in every field of technology. The United States will be the world leader in some fields, Germany in others, France in still others. Japan will best assert a high profile in technological development by asserting focused strengths.

COMMONALITY

Overly self-contained R&D programs at individual companies are the third reason for Japan's inefficiency in using human resources in R&D. Conducting core R&D programs internally and confidentially is natural and necessary in a highly competitive environment. What is neither natural nor necessary is Japanese companies' practice of conducting even most of their basic research internally and thereby minimizing the commonality among R&D activity at different companies.

Granted, the borderline between basic research and applied research can be difficult to distinguish precisely. But a large realm of scientific research is indisputably "basic"—not specific to any individual product-development project. That research is the foundation for all technological development, and increasing the commonality of that research among companies will raise efficiency in R&D at every company.

Japan's lack of commonality in basic research among companies is attributable to lifetime employment and to seniority-based compensation. Traditional employment practices have limited the occupational mobility of researchers and engineers among Japanese companies. Greater mobility surely would have resulted in greater commonality in basic research. It would have enabled companies to achieve greater results in R&D with smaller allocations of personnel and funding.

The end of lifetime employment thus offers the potential for raising productivity in Japanese R&D, but it also presents a huge challenge. That challenge is the task of maintaining smooth continuity in corporate R&D programs.

Traditionally, researchers and engineers at Japanese companies have learned their trade largely on the job and under the guidance of their seniors and superiors. They have inherited R&D projects from their predecessors, and they have been able to step in and carry on the work without dropping a beat. Japanese companies commonly adhere to personnel rotation schedules irrespective of the status of R&D projects under way. Manufacturers rotate R&D personnel at project stages where a change of personnel would be terribly disruptive and therefore unthinkable at a U.S. or European company.

The Japanese companies can afford to rotate personnel freely because lifetime employment has nurtured a thorough sharing of knowledge and perspectives. That internal commonality and the flexibility that it permits in deploying human resources rank among the few advantages of the traditional Japanese approach. In that regard, the end of lifetime employment could therefore diminish efficiency and raise costs for Japanese companies in R&D.

Japanese industry needs to ensure that the R&D-related benefits of the end of lifetime employment outweigh the drawbacks. A strong and shared foundation of basic research will support higher efficiency in R&D. Integrating that foundation into the social infrastructure and establishing broadly based mechanisms for propagating scientific research will help maintain the smooth succession in R&D inside companies.

The strengthened and shared foundation of basic research will reside primarily in Japan's universities and in public-sector research institutes. Those centers of research have hitherto concentrated almost exclusively on scientific work and have largely avoided involvement in commercially applicable technological development. Personnel interchange with corporate R&D programs has been minimal. The end of lifetime employment will occasion increased mobility for university and public-sector researchers, as well as for their corporate counterparts. A freer flow of people and ideas will raise the standard of research in science and technology.

Companies are fiercely protective of their intellectual property, and they work systematically to maintain the confidentiality of research findings. Corporate executives will frown on the outflow of information that will accompany the growing mobility of R&D personnel. Their best response, however, will be to foster social infrastructure for accumulating and building on the best ideas from every company, university, and public-sector research institute. That will reduce R&D costs for industry and strengthen Japan's overall capabilities in technological development.

A NEW SYSTEM OF CORPORATE MANAGEMENT

Japanese manufacturing has benefited incalculably from the employee loyalty engendered by lifetime employment and seniority-based compensation. So what happens to the competitiveness of Japanese manufacturing when the traditional mode of employment collapses, when Japanese companies encounter the same issues that have bedeviled their U.S. and European counterparts for years? What new methods of production control will become necessary to motivate employees and to maintain internationally competitive quality and productivity in an era of unprecedented labor mobility?

Simply maintaining adequate communication inside companies will require increased attention to the methods of communication and will entail increased cost. Japanese companies, having abandoned the internally shared values and shared understanding inculcated by lifetime employment, will need to adopt increasingly systematic management. That same need underlay the development of scientific management in the United States. Witness the ubiquity of university graduate programs in business administration there and the hoards of MBA holders spawned by those programs.

The distribution of wealth is far more unequal in the United States than in Japan, and U.S. society is a veritable rainbow of ethnicity and culture, together with a correspondingly vast spectrum of values. Assembling teams of employees from disparate backgrounds and inducing those teams to create quality products efficiently is an incredible challenge. The end of lifetime employment will present Japanese companies with a similar task. Corporate managers in Japan will not encounter anything like the social diversity that their American counterparts face, but coping with the new challenge will nonetheless demand a lot more than mere rules of thumb.

Japanese management will need to do more than simply find new ways to motivate employees. Companies will need to revamp their production systems and realign their organizations to accommodate the new realities. Designing and operating new production-control systems will require new skills and expertise. Companies will increasingly need to supplement internally cultivated human resources with mid-career specialists recruited in the labor market. They will contend with a dearth of the needed specialists for the time being. Japanese industry has not hitherto provided much of a market for such human resources. The U.S. system of MBA education and employment warrants careful study and possible emulation in Japan.

Capital spending will need to reflect the changes in employee attitudes and the new approaches to production control. A substantial decline in worker motivation, for example, would increase the number of employees required to operate the same amount of equipment. Japan's shrinking workforce will oblige industry to reduce its stock of plant and equipment.

The reduction in plant and equipment might need to be even bigger than the shrinkage in the workforce. A changing work ethic, that is, could affect the level of capital intensiveness that is suitable for Japanese industry. In addition, the new production-control systems will presumably entail higher costs. That will raise the break-even point for companies, which will lower return on investment and force managements to become more circumspect in capital spending.

Corporate management will thus become increasingly complex in the shrinking-population economy. To repeat, the shrinking and aging of the population need not render industry unprofitable. But those trends do mean that industry needs to adopt new strategies and new systems quickly to remain profitable.

ABOUT JAPANESE MANUFACTURERS' OVERSEAS PRODUCTION

Some readers are surely growing impatient with the author for focusing exclusively on Japan in discussing the availability of labor and trends in demand. Yes, the Japanese workforce and Japanese demand will shrink. But Japanese manufacturers can continue growing by expanding their production in other nations. Yet their investment in global manufacturing could accelerate the shrinkage of the Japanese economy. That result would occur if and to the extent that the Japanese manufacturers financed their overseas investment with funds raised in Japan.

Diverting funds to overseas investment projects would reduce the amount of domestic savings available to finance investment in Japan. That would diminish the stock of plant and equipment in Japan, increase unemployment, and lower national income.

Rarely have Japanese companies financed overseas investment projects entirely with funds raised outside Japan. Considerations of investment risk and funding cost prompt them to finance a big part of their overseas investment with internal funding. And that reduces the amount of retained earnings available for investment in Japan.

Even if financed entirely with overseas funding, Japanese manufacturers' international investment would contribute little to income levels in Japan. The attendant value-added would arise mainly outside Japan and would accrue chiefly in the host nations. Individual companies headquartered in Japan can grow by expanding abroad. But their international expansion is unlikely to add much to Japanese income levels.

This issue has much in common with the much-bemoaned threat of the "hollowing" of Japanese industry—the flight of manufacturing and of related technology to lower-wage environments. Japan maintains a basically free and open investment framework, however, so government policy measures for somehow corralling corporate investment are out of the question. Rather, Japanese need to account for outward capital spending in their economic planning.

The author believes, incidentally, that overseas investment by Japanese manufacturers is unlikely to increase dramatically. Japan's most internationally competitive companies will continue to expand their operations around the world. But they are likely to be exceptions to the rule for Japanese industry overall.

Companies endure a host of handicaps in setting up manufacturing operations outside their home nations. They contend with shortages of information in general, and they encounter unfamiliar political systems and cultural environments. The attendant risk seems certain to dissuade most Japanese manufacturers from internationalizing their production greatly. Meanwhile, Japanese imports from Japanese-owned production operations overseas reduce demand for domestic production. That will diminish enthusiasm for overseas investment at companies that are striving to maintain the viability of domestic manufacturing operations.

A GROWTH INDUSTRY FOR THE SHRINKING-POPULATION ECONOMY

We need to acknowledge the differentials between companies—even in the same industry—when we cite the need for downsizing in step with Japan's shrinking workforce and shrinking demand. Overall demand in the Japanese economy and the overall size of the Japanese workforce are easier to project accurately than the amounts of plant and equipment and the numbers of employees that individual companies will require.

Corporate managements confront a bewildering universe of variables, and the uncertainty about long-term needs for plant and equipment will only increase in the shrinking-population economy. One useful tool for coping with that uncertainty will be leasing. Construction companies already use leasing extensively to obtain equipment for individual projects without incurring investment risk. (Here, we are referring to so-called operating leases, which are essentially rentals, as opposed to financing leases, which are essentially a form of financing capital spending.) Other manufacturers will also be able to reduce their investment risk by obtaining production equipment through leasing.

Overall investment in equipment for leasing to companies in an industry can reflect projections for demand in that industry. Those projections will tend to be more reliable than projections for plant-and-equipment needs at individual companies. Leasing will thus allow for distributing risk among companies. It will help optimize capital spending in the Japanese economy overall. International expansion by the leasing industry would allow for distributing risk and for optimizing capital spending over an even-broader terrain.

Leasing is exactly the kind of business that can and should grow spontaneously in the private sector of the shrinking-population economy. Lessors will be ideally positioned to provide lessees with optimally priced equipment and to provide them with useful advice.

RESTRUCTURING REGIONAL ECONOMIC SYSTEMS

LOCALLY GENERATED INCOME

D emographic aging will proceed far slower in Japan's outlying prefectures than in and around its main metropolitan areas. Meanwhile, the focus of Japanese industry is shifting to consumer goods, from capital goods. That shift will tend to decentralize production and to thereby stimulate industrial vitality outside Japan's highly industrialized urban regions.

Fulfilling the potential for economic vitalization in Japan's outlying regions will depend, however, on employing labor optimally. Japan's nonurban prefectures will need to establish frameworks for employing labor in ways that increase their autonomous earning capacity and that reduce their industrial and economic reliance on the nation's metropolitan regions. That will need to include realigning the geographic division of labor in Japanese industry.

Note that revenue-sharing programs for redistributing tax revenues have the same effect as expanding local industry in increasing local income. Likewise, public works spending, a traditional economic mainstay of Japan's nonmetropolitan prefectures, also increases local incomes. Both of these sources of income will shrink greatly, however, as overall tax revenues decline and as funding for new public works projects dries up. Those trends amplify the need for self-sustaining industrial development in each region of the nation.

Note, too, that the growth in service industries is no panacea for Japan's outlying prefectures in regard to economic vitalization. The service sector accounts for a growing share of economic activity throughout Japan, and that share will continue to rise as the aging of society presents mounting demand for services. Business in services tends to be geographically self-contained, however, and therefore does not attract inflows of revenues.

Service vendors and their customers all reside in the same region, so their transactions consist of simply circulating funds locally. The seed money needs to come from other sources. In Japan's present industrial framework, that means from the highly industrialized metropolitan regions. Growth in the service sector, meanwhile, reduces the amount of labor available for manufacturing.

REGIONAL GROUPINGS

Redressing the geographical imbalance in Japanese industry will require more than simply relocating factories to the less-industrialized prefectures. That's because manufacturing activity relies on a comprehensive range of planning and design, marketing, administrative, and other support functions, and those functions reside mainly in the principal industrial centers.

For Japan's outlying prefectures to increase their autonomous earnings potential, they need to attract a full range of industrial functions. No single prefecture can host a range of functions large enough to support self-sustaining industrial development. Geographically contiguous prefectures will need to build complementary industrial platforms that, together, constitute autonomous industrial centers. In addition to the complementation among prefectures in individual regional centers, complementation among regional centers can contribute to realigning Japan's geographic division of labor.

Specialization will be crucial. The regional centers will need to focus rigorously on selected product categories and will need to purchase other products from other regions. Specialization is essential to the principle of promoting economic flows among regions. It is also essential to industrial competitiveness. Undertaking an overly broad range of product categories would dilute the regions' hard-won competitive strengths.

Carefully focused industrial development will allow the regions to build competitive strengths in technological development, as well as in economies of scale. Maintaining that focus will be indispensable in fostering autonomous industrial centers that are credible rivals to Japan's metropolitan regions.

Specialization will increase the competitiveness of Japanese industry overall, as well as strengthening the industrial competitiveness of individual regions. That is because enterprises and regions will focus on industries of comparative advantage, and resources will withdraw from industries of comparative disadvantage. Japan will finally unburden itself of a longstanding commitment to far too many uncompetitive industries.

Different kinds of specialization are possible. Apart from the obvious option of specializing in selected products and industries, regions can also foster specialized strengths in selected stages of production processes. Vigorous economic interchange among prefectures and among regions will be the rule, since specializations are by nature complementary. That interaction will maximize the prospects for reducing prefectures' industrial reliance on Japan's three largest metropolitan areas. Regional economic groupings will soon acquire highly competitive strengths. For example, their geography alone can support compelling advantages in logistics.

THREE ISSUES FOR REGIONAL ECONOMIC GROUPINGS

Fulfilling the potential of regional economic groupings for revitalizing Japan's outlying prefectures will depend on addressing three issues. One, any new architecture for regional governance will need to conform with the geography of the regional economic groupings. Two, prefectures will need to work systematically to foster and retain the human resources that will be indispensable to regional economic development. Three, the industrial infrastructure is on the verge of collapse in some prefectures, and special measures will be necessary to ensure that it survives until the regional economic groupings begin to generate benefits.

Japanese are debating a sweeping range of tax reforms and other measures for devolving government authority and for promoting fiscal equilibrium among the nation's prefectures. Whatever the merits of those measures, their effectiveness will hinge on accommodating the geography of the new regional economic groupings. A geographical mismatch between administrative jurisdictions and economic groupings would be counterproductive. Japanese need to wait until the geography of the economic groupings becomes clear before finalizing any architecture for regional governance.

People in Japan's less-industrialized prefectures bemoan a "brain drain." The most-capable human resources, they say, tend to drift to the nation's largest metropolitan areas. That threatens to undermine those prefectures' capacity for tackling the challenges of fostering R&D capabilities and building regional economic groupings. The prefectures in question therefore need to move forthrightly to put in place systems for fostering and retaining human resources.

Building and upgrading universities will be a good place to begin. That's because a big part of the outflow of human resources occurs when young people leave home to attend out-of-prefecture universities. Along with strengthening local university systems, the prefectures should develop complementary institutions for providing advanced and practical education in technology and management. Focusing higher-education resources strategically on skills and knowledge essential to selected industries is an approach that warrants consideration. That approach will be most effective if it transcends individual prefectures and addresses the development strategies of regional economic groupings. The employment opportunities generated by those groupings, meanwhile, will reinforce the constituent prefectures' appeal for well-qualified human resources.

As for concerns about the survival of industrial infrastructure in outlying prefectures, those concerns have ample justification. Industrial infrastructure has deteriorated alarmingly in some prefectures. Changes in the composition of demand and in the structure of Japan's workforce will, as noted, work in favor of industrially undeveloped prefectures. But whether the industrial infrastructure in those prefectures can survive long enough to benefit from those changes is questionable. A strategy of concentrating prefectural and regional resources on selected industries will work only if infrastructure exists to support those industries.

Figure 37 provides a useful perspective on which prefectures present the most-pressing need for measures to shore up their industrial infrastructure. It contrasts industrial growth with economic dependence on public works spending. The vertical axis indicates manufacturing output by prefecture and metropolitan area in 1995 as a multiple of the figure

Figure 37

Growth in Manufacturing Output and Dependence on Public Works Spending

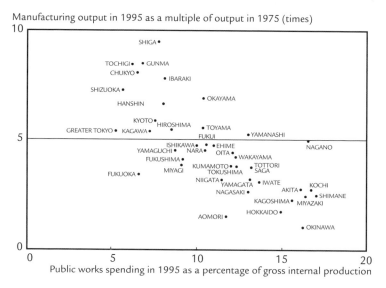

Source: Prefectural economic data published by the Economic Planning Agency
(now part of the Cabinet Office)

for 1975, and the horizontal axis indicates public works spending as a percentage of gross internal production in 1995. The industries that earn net inflows of cash are mainly in the manufacturing sector. Sluggish growth in that sector signifies a deteriorating economic foundation. Similarly, a high dependence on public works spending signifies vulnerability to the impending decline in that spending. The further prefectures appear toward the lower right in figure 37, the more pressing is their need for fortifying industrial infrastructure.

NEW APPROACHES TO PUBLIC WORKS PROJECTS

Note that the dots in figure 37 form a band that angles downward from left to right. That is a reflection of Japanese industrial policy. The government has allocated public works spending to prefectures and metropolitan areas roughly in inverse proportion to their industrial growth rates. Note, too, that economic dependence on public works projects is even greater than the figure indicates. Some of the production output recorded under other categories is in fulfillment of demand generated by those projects.

The national government has a natural interest in minimizing the economic differentials among prefectures. And public works projects are, for all intents and purposes, a function of national government budgeting. Prefectures nominally foot the bill for the portion of public works projects not covered directly by national-government subsidies. But they fund that spending mainly with their allocations from Japan's revenue-sharing program.

Public works projects, however, are an inappropriate means of narrowing geographic economic differentials. Those projects are properly for creating and upgrading infrastructure to support economic and social progress. The conspicuous linkage of public works spending to economic growth rates, however, exposes a profound deviance from that ostensible purpose. That perversion of fiscal policy has distorted the structure of industry in the recipient prefectures. It has fostered an industrial dependence on the fiscal handouts distributed through public works projects, and it has thereby aggravated the deterioration of the prefectures' economic foundations. The construction industry and peripheral industries have become bloated while other industries—including industries that could ordinarily grow independently and earn inflows of cash—have withered.

Public works spending will decline sharply and unavoidably, so the time has come to refocus that spending on its proper purpose. The government needs to choose projects carefully and devote priority to those that will help support a shrunken and aged society. In choosing projects, the government also needs to account for the changing economic balance among Japan's regions.

Postwar public works spending in Japan concentrated initially on developing industrial zones in Japan's three largest metropolitan areas. Its focus subsequently shifted to redistributing the wealth that arose in those areas evenly throughout the nation. The new focus was evident in Japan's Second Comprehensive National Land Development Plan (Shinzenso), adopted in 1969. That plan provided for building extensive transport networks of freeways and Shinkansen bullet trains to broaden the geographical potential for industrial development. Even today, Japan continues to expand those networks in accordance with the basic outlines of the 1969 plan.

Huge and still-growing transport networks have failed, however, to increase the capacity of Japan's outlying regions to achieve autonomous economic growth. Figure 37 reveals a strong and persistent relationship between the growth rate in manufacturing and proximity to the three largest metropolitan areas. Japan's transport networks expanded greatly during the two decades—1975 to 1995—covered in the graph.

Freeways and Shinkansen lines shortened the transport times between Japan's outlying prefectures and its three largest metropolitan areas. But that shortening had the opposite effect of what Japan's policy makers intended. It increased the efficiency of logistics centered on the metropolitan areas and thus increased the reach of manufacturing industries in those areas. In other words, the expanded transport networks benefited the metropolitan areas more than they benefited the outlying areas. They had the net effect of amplifying industrial and economic disparity.

In any case, economic planning oriented toward redistributing wealth accumulated in Japan's three largest metropolitan areas is anachronistic. The relative weighting of those areas in Japan's economy will decline unavoidably. Economic growth and revitalization for Japan's outlying prefectures will depend on increasing the economic self-sufficiency of those prefectures. That will need to include building regional economic groupings.

The kind of infrastructure required to promote regional economic integration is not massive networks centered on Japan's metropolitan areas. What are needed are highways and other infrastructure for supporting interchange among groups of contiguous prefectures. So accommodating an economic structure characterized by regional economic groupings will demand a completely new approach to infrastructure. And that infrastructure will be surprisingly less expensive than traditional infrastructure. It will be entirely affordable even under Japan's declining budget for public works spending.

Regional transport networks need not necessarily entail building freeways or other kinds of new infrastructure. Shaving minutes off of transport times will be comparatively unimportant in the short distances characteristic of regional logistics. Upgrading the existing networks of national and prefectural highways will suffice for most purposes. Nor will Japan need much in the way of new industrial parks. Plenty of space for new projects is available in the nation's existing industrial concentrations.

Something that will be especially important in the new infrastructure model is sound approaches to residential development. Measures to raise productivity will include regional convergences of production resources, and that is likely to result in big population shifts inside prefectures and inside multi-prefecture regions. Formerly, insufficient attention to housing policy occasioned overconcentrations of population in residential parts of Japan's big cities and suburban sprawl on their perimeters. Japanese need to learn from those mistakes and provide well-planned tracts of public and private housing in the new regional centers. Before undertaking new industrial developments, prefectures need to enact zoning laws for enforcing an appropriate division between industrial and residential land use and to build rental public housing. Development plans also need to devote ample attention, of course, to providing services for elderly residents.

FISCAL WOES FOR CITIES

Population shrinkage and aging present especially daunting fiscal issues for Japan's cities. High population density is a defining characteristic of cities, and rising population density entails costs. Cities damage the natural environment. Urban congestion impedes the movement of people and goods, and it can even be dangerous. Concentrations of population and industry drive real estate prices upward. These and other problems are costs that, left unmanaged, reduce the effectiveness of basic city functions. Offsetting the above problems and maintaining city functions are activities that also entail costs: building and repair work undertaken by the municipalities on streets, parks, sewers, and public housing, along with urban redevelopment projects undertaken by the private sector.

Maintaining cities is thus a costly proposition. But cities continue to grow because they generate value-added that greatly exceeds the cost of their maintenance. Their concentrations of labor and industry support highly efficient manufacturing, and that in turn supports the growth of tertiary industries, which increases the cities' value-added further. Urbanites enjoy a wealth of employment opportunities and of convenience—advantages that result from urban value-added.

Population shrinkage and aging, however, threaten to undermine the fiscal viability of cities. Demographic aging will proceed faster in Japan's large cities than in its small regional cities or in the countryside, but population decline will occur more slowly in the large cities than elsewhere. Urban populations will age rapidly because of the convergence of young people in the cities that has continued for decades—a convergence that will now end naturally because of the shrinkage of Japan's population.

The cost of maintaining Japan's large cities will remain high and will possibly even increase. Japan's urban populations will shrink slowly for the time being, and municipalities will need to spend heavily on services and infrastructure for the swelling ranks of elderly residents. Large concentrations of elderly people, by the way, are a characteristic of large cities in all nations. The cost of supporting those elderly concentrations is thus inherent to urban administration.

On the other side of the fiscal equation, urban finances in Japan will also suffer from declining revenues. A shrinking workforce will reduce the total value-added generated in Japan, but the decline in value-added will be especially sharp in the nation's large cities. That is because the rapid aging of urban workforces will depress productivity.

The larger the cities, the larger will be the worsening of the fiscal balance. Municipal finances will reflect the rise in urban costs and the decline in urban value-added. Fiscal surpluses will narrow steadily. Some cities will fall into deficit. Maintaining public services will become increasingly difficult. Urban redevelopment projects will become increasingly unattractive as investments. Japan's cities will deteriorate. Once-prosperous neighborhoods will turn into slums.

A PREFECTURAL PERSPECTIVE ON URBAN FINANCES

Predicting the fiscal future of individual cities to any meaningful degree of accuracy is impossible. Movements of population are a far-greater variable at the city level than at the geographically broader prefectural level. The relative fiscal effect of relocating factories, for example, is larger for individual cities than for their prefectures. In any case, city limits rarely define the boundaries of the distribution of production capacity or labor. So we will obtain more-useful insight into the fiscal prospects for Japan's cities by adopting a prefectural perspective.

Figure 38 verifies our suspicion that municipal finances will deteriorate most severely in Japan's largest metropolitan areas. The vertical axis

Figure 38
Municipal Vicissitudes: Change from 1998 to 2030

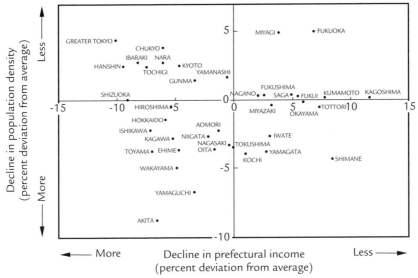

Source: Projections by the author

in the graph indicates the amount of decline in population density between 1998 and 2030, and the horizontal axis indicates the amount of decline in real prefectural income over the same span. The author has plotted each prefecture and region according to its deviation from the average. Urban costs reflect population density, and the amount of relative decline—or lack of decline—in those costs tends to mirror trends in population density. Prefectural income, meanwhile, is gross income—total value-added generated—per prefecture or region, not per capita. The further a prefecture or region appears to the upper left in the graph, the more its fiscal position is likely to deteriorate.

As we would expect, Tokyo appears likely to suffer the worst fiscal deterioration, followed by Japan's other large metropolitan areas and by prefectures on the periphery of the large metropolitan areas. These are regions where population shrinkage will be smaller than in other parts of the nation, which minimizes the potential for a decline in urban costs. So declines in prefectural income, aggravated by the rapid aging of workforces, will affect prefectural finances severely. The rapidity of aging in these regions could occasion an even-greater fiscal deterioration than we might surmise from the graph.

In contrast, the fiscal condition of prefectures at the lower right in figure 38 will deteriorate only slightly or will possibly even improve. Even the prefectures at the lower left in the figure could remain fiscally healthy. Large declines in population density might lower their fiscal costs enough or even more than enough to offset the declines in prefectural income.

Bear in mind, however, that we are examining fiscal prospects at the prefectural and multi-prefectural level. Positioning in the lower right and elsewhere in the lower part of figure 38 is fiscally reassuring for prefectures, but it does not necessarily imply a similarly promising outlook for individual cities. The populations of some cities in the prefectures in the lower part of the graph will shrink severely. That shrinkage could be so severe in some cities as to render them unviable. Cities require a critical mass of population to function as urban units. Where populations shrink to a size smaller than that critical mass, cities could become ghost towns.

RETHINKING URBAN MAINTENANCE

Population shrinkage and aging demand new perspectives on urban maintenance. They especially require new approaches to investment for increasing the efficiency of urban functions. In an expanding-population economy, constructing high-rise buildings to maximize land-use efficiency makes sense. Building roads to reduce time costs makes sense, too. Those kinds of investment increase cities' capacity for generating value-added. But a shrinking-population economy obliges urban planners to devote careful attention to the effects of investment on urban costs, as well as on value-added. Ill-conceived investment can aggravate the problem of depopulation and increase urban costs even as it raises urban efficiency.

Urban planners also need to consider the future expenditures on maintenance that proposed building projects, including private-sector projects, will require. Cities of shrinking populations will generate less value-added in the future than they generate today. Buildings will fall into disrepair and large swaths of urban architecture will become decrepit as funding for maintenance becomes insufficient.

City administrators thus need to consider long-term fiscal trends in weighing the lifetime costs and benefits of projects. They also need to develop new methods of city management. Japan has tended to address needs by building new infrastructure even where regulations would serve the same purpose less expensively. Well-conceived traffic regulations, for example, can be just as effective as widening streets and boulevards in maintaining smooth flows of people and goods. Restricting the entry of large vehicles can be more effective than widening roadways in addressing the costs of environmental degradation and deteriorating safety.

Also warranting attention are the hidden costs of investment projects for raising urban efficiency. A project that attracts concentrations of traffic, for instance, can necessitate new and widened roadways. This is further reason for city officials to scrutinize private-sector projects, as well as public-sector undertakings, from the perspective of the effect on municipal finances.

Another issue presented by population shrinkage and aging is the need for determining where to allocate limited resources for maintaining urban functions. Numerous small cities in Japan host public-sector projects far larger than the cities' populations and economies would seem to warrant. Those projects take place partly because the host municipalities bear little of the cost of financing the projects and partly because large-scale projects are necessary to generate the desired economic benefits. They will become untenable, however, in the shrinking-population economy.

Throughout Japan, villages, towns, and cities are merging to reduce redundancy in administrative expenditures and to offset fiscal surpluses against fiscal deficits. Today's surpluses, however, will decline and sometimes even become deficits amid population shrinkage and aging. The municipal and government officials responsible for realigning units of local government need to evaluate long-term fiscal trends and coordinate their activities accordingly. Their evaluation needs to include a readiness to recognize that some towns and cities will simply become unviable.

We have seen that population in Japan's outlying prefectures will concentrate increasingly in regional cities. Those regional hubs are the natural and appropriate focus for allocating increasingly scarce public funds to fortify urban functions.

Lifestyle Planning in a Shrinking Population

Increasing Diversity

Growing numbers of Japanese will increase their earning power by acquiring and honing specialized professional skills. Some will devote themselves assiduously to a single specialty for their entire careers, starting when they are still in school. Others will walk away from unsatisfying work and go back to school to gain new and more-rewarding skills. Some will move from company to company to acquire experience useful for their chosen specialties. The end of seniority-based compensation will eliminate the penalty for changing employers. Opportunities will abound for people to move up to higher compensation curves by receiving advanced education or by accumulating valuable real-world experience.

Traditionally, Japanese working people have acquired specialties through on-the-job training under the guidance of their seniors. Japanese are entirely serious in admonishing young people to "forget what you learned in school when you go to work in the real world." Each company has its own way of doing things, and the specialties that employees learn on the job are highly specific to their companies. The specialized capabilities of a standout employee at Toyota—whether on the production line or in the office—are not necessarily transferable to Nissan.

Specialized skills will become more universal and more transferable among companies as lifetime employment and seniority-based compensation collapse. School and university education and training will play a growing role in preparing people for the workplace. To fulfill that role, educational institutions will need to revise their curricula, and the education system will require realignment.

Meanwhile, Japanese will increasingly exercise "the freedom not to work." We saw in the previous chapter that the number of freeters—free arbeiters: workers who eschew long-term commitments to employers—is growing in Japan. That number will continue to grow as Japanese encounter a broadening diversity of work and lifestyle options. Relatively unskilled freeters, as we have seen, will need to subsist at the low end of the wage spectrum. Highly skilled workers, however, will enjoy high compensation and unprecedented freedom.

A growing number of Japanese will opt for simple lifestyles. Japanese will learn the lessons of their American counterparts: that high-pressure careers entail higher divorce rates and shorter life spans, that pursuing raises and promotions is not necessarily the route to happiness. Curtailing expenditures on material goods and rediscovering nonmaterial pleasures will increase the freedom not work.

A vast range of new values will come into play in shaping Japanese lifestyles. Changes in the pension system, along with changes in modes of employment, will fuel the growth in lifestyle diversity. We don't know exactly how sweeping the pension system changes will be, so we cannot predict confidently how much they will influence lifestyles. We can be certain, however, that Japanese will need to take more responsibility for their postretirement finances. Pensions will be insufficient to support everyone in their old age.

Lifetime employment and seniority-based compensation, together with generous pension benefits, freed people from the need for rigorous financial planning. Henceforth, people will need to devote careful attention during their working years to providing for their postretirement livelihoods. And longer life spans mean more postretirement years to provide for. Everyone will need to give careful thought to how and where they want to pass their time after retirement. They will need to put aside enough savings to fulfill their postretirement plans.

A recent survey found that more than 60% of Americans look forward to retirement and that a majority of Europeans also anticipate retirement in a positive vein. The same survey found that fewer than 30% of Japanese look forward to retirement. Japanese anxiety about retirement, the author suspects, reflects a lack of personal planning. Concrete notions of where you want to be and what you want to be doing after retirement are a prerequisite for positive anticipation. Japan's shrinking-population economy poses a host of challenges, but it also offers unprecedented freedom of choice. Japanese need to discover and assert that freedom, especially in regard to the latter part of their increasingly long lives.

DIVERSITY IN COMPETITION, TOO

Changes in modes of work will affect patterns of competition in society. A good example is the competition for places in prestigious universities.

That competition is so intense that Japanese commonly liken it to war. The reason for the intensity is that Japanese companies weigh the prominence of job applicants' universities heavily in hiring. Graduates of "good universities" enjoy higher compensation and higher social status than graduates of lesser universities throughout their working lives. The end of lifetime employment and of seniority-based compensation will diminish that premium and alleviate the pressure on high school students to gain acceptance to prominent universities.

Under lifetime employment and seniority-based compensation, companies nurture human resources on the job at the hands of older employees. Graduation from a prominent university signifies that a person possesses the potential to become— through on-the-job training—a productive employee. The collective management and group dynamics characteristic of Japanese companies, meanwhile, have minimized the importance of highly specialized skills. So a diploma from a prestigious university has been a ticket to a lifetime of preferential treatment. And since Japanese universities graduate nearly everyone that they admit, students obtain that ticket the moment they gain acceptance.

The end of lifetime employment and of seniority-based compensation will leave specialized competence as the chief criterion for determining compensation and promotions. The name of the university that a person attended will become less important than what he or she learned there. A background in general studies will not qualify many graduates for premium salaries. Traditional on-the-job training will go the way of lifetime employment, and employees will compete for compensation and position on the basis of the skills they acquired before joining their companies. The value that accrues from simply having gained admission to a prestigious university will dissolve.

Note that all this will change the ground rules for social competition profoundly in yet another way. Sports furnish a useful metaphor. A baseball team, for example, focuses on different skill sets in evaluating prospective players for different positions. Outfielders do not compete against pitchers for spots on the team. Outfielders compete with outfielders, pitchers with pitchers, and so on.

Japan has been like a baseball team that uses a single set of selection criteria for players at every position. Its focus on university hierarchy has favored the people most skilled in taking the entrance examinations—

entrance examinations for the universities and for the secondary schools, elementary schools, and even kindergartens that prepare students most effectively to pass the university entrance examinations.

A single skill set—skills in passing entrance examinations—has been the sole focus of Japanese competition for high-paying jobs and high social status. The system has handicapped otherwise-competent individuals whose strengths do not happen to include test-taking skills. It has robbed industry and society of the services of those individuals in positions where they could have excelled. The emerging emphasis on specialized skills will diversify the routes that lead to success in society. Outfielders will no longer need to compete with pitchers for spots on the team.

Competition, to be sure, will remain intense. But it will become less arbitrary and less narrow. Japanese will enjoy an unprecedented range of opportunities to compete for the jobs and careers of their choice. As seniority-based compensation gives way to performance-based compensation and as job hopping becomes common, people will be able to give full play to their capabilities. Losing in any single round of competition will not be fatal. Alternative opportunities will always be on offer.

The flip side of this transformation will be growing inequality. Japan's narrow emphasis on gaining acceptance to prestigious universities has undoubtedly been unhealthy for individuals and for society at large. On the other hand, the differentials in compensation and in social status between the system's winners and losers have been small by Western standards. The winner-take-all principle will prevail in the new competitive framework. That principle is familiar in professional sports, where star players earn far more than benchwarmers. Japan, however, will no longer relegate individuals arbitrarily to the bench for a lifetime. Everyone will enjoy continuing opportunities to compete for spots in the starting lineup. That increase in opportunity will be a hallmark of the shrinking-population economy.

WHITHER "WE JAPANESE"?

Japan has benefited immensely from offering its citizens the promise of economic progress and from making good on that promise. Nearly everyone has enjoyed continuing gains in income during their working lives. The certainty of economic progress has engendered a powerful sense of national unity. That sense of unity, even more than the much-cited factors of ethnic homogeneity and narrow income differentials, is responsible for Japan's vaunted social tranquility.

The propensity of Japanese to refer to "we Japanese" reflects a genuine solidarity, and the roots of that solidarity are economic. Japanese have perceived a direct connection between their nation's economic performance and continuing gains in their standards of living. Rare is the nation where the economic growth rate figures so commonly in conversation as in Japan. Broader social issues and even community matters take a back seat to economic concerns in Japan. And most Japanese have participated in the economy through their membership in the social microcosms known as companies.

Japan's GDP, in itself, will become an increasingly weak foundation for maintaining a sense of national unity. Even on a per capita basis, the economy will cease growing and could begin to shrink somewhat. The unavoidable reduction in pension benefits will broaden income differentials between working-age people and retirees. No longer will Japanese be able to take for granted continuing gains in living standards.

Japanese will possess growing quantities of one important asset, however, even in the absence of economic growth. That asset is leisure time. Technological progress will continue to raise labor productivity, and reduced rates of capital spending will allow for sharing a growing portion of industrial value-added with workers. The increase in leisure, therefore, will be a tangible result of economic progress. Japanese will presumably continue to regard their nation's economy as a wellspring of abundance. They will presumably retain a strong-enough sense of national unity to ensure continuing social tranquility.

Increased leisure, though, will mean increased opportunity for people to explore individual interests, and a new individualism will arise. Whereas the common pursuit of economic growth enforced shared values, the mutual enjoyment of leisure will foster a growing diversity of values. The vantage of "I" will replace the perspective of "we Japanese." People will begin to regard themselves more as members of their community than as citizens of the nation.

Maximizing the social benefits of increased leisure will require suitable spaces for enjoying leisure pursuits. Entertainment and amusement facilities are part of the answer. But far more important will be parks, plazas, and other spaces where people can gather freely for any purpose and at no charge. Japanese cities have grown and developed largely as platforms for supporting economic activity. Their streets and office buildings, moderated only by establishments for eating, drinking, and shopping, hardly encourage residents or visitors to simply relax and revel in thought.

Japanese can learn a lot from the European tradition of interspersing plazas through the urban landscape. But city planning will need to accommodate local culture and traditions and local patterns of leisure. Japanese will then enjoy the virtuous circle of increased leisure begetting community spirit and community spirit begetting a broadening spectrum of opportunities for enjoying leisure. Here again, Japan's shrinking-population economy offers the exciting promise of richer, more-fulfilling lives. The task for Japanese policy makers is to ensure the fulfillment of that promise while coping with the fiscal and social challenges of profound demographic change.

Postscript

The author has endeavored in this work to highlight the central role of diversity in Japan's shrinking-population economy. Population shrinkage and aging will occasion increased diversity in economic activity. And diverse economic behavior will be the best response to demographic change. That change will put an end to lifetime employment and seniority-based compensation. In their place will arise the freedom not to work, which will engender explosive diversity in modes of employment, in lifestyles, in values.

Life will become more interesting. Income levels might not keep rising, but people will enjoy an unprecedented range of choice. And they will have an unprecedented amount of leisure time to consider and explore their options.

Industry will also display a new diversity. Management policies have been numbingly monotonous as corporations have pursued the common goal of increasing sales volume. A widespread corporate shift of focus toward increasing value-added will stimulate originality in products and technology. It will dilute the traditional premium associated with size. Small will become (at least potentially) beautiful.

Regional diversity will multiply, too. Demographic aging will proceed more slowly in Japan's outlying prefectures than in its large metropolitan areas. Those prefectures will presumably augment their economic potential further by forging regional economic groupings. The metropolises, meanwhile, will need to serve their growing concentrations of elderly residents while coping with deteriorating fiscal positions.

A new fiscal perspective will become necessary at the national level, too. Raising taxes would only aggravate the economic challenges posed by population shrinkage and aging. The government needs to refocus and narrow its public works spending and other expenditures sufficiently to remain solvent without raising taxes.

Some bureaucrats seem to feel responsible for sketching suitable directions for personal and corporate economic behavior in the era of demographic shrinkage and aging. The whole point of diversity, however, is that individuals and companies assume responsibility for mapping their own futures. Japan's bureaucrats would do better to concentrate on fortifying a suitable infrastructure to support independent decisions by the nation's citizenry and industry. Small government is essential to social and economic vitality in a shrinking and aging population.

A WORD ABOUT LIFE ON THE LAND

"Returning to nature" figures prominently among the lifestyle options in industrialized nations. Japanese have generally denigrated that option as utopian, but their prejudice reflects an unhealthy fixation on industrialization and urbanization. The Netherlands, with a population density every bit the equal of Japan's, maintains sweeping pastoral expanses on its interior while positioning metropolises on the periphery.

Japanese agriculture, to be sure, is unproductive by international standards. But that is partly due to arbitrary regulatory restrictions on ownership of agricultural land. It is also partly due to the overly narrow focus of policies for promoting agriculture. Promoting related industries, such as agricultural machinery and fertilizer, along with farming could nurture economic synergies. Those synergies would arise most readily in regional economic groupings larger than individual prefectures.

Let us also note the potential value of agriculture in engaging members of an aging workforce gainfully. This is not to suggest for a moment that agricultural employment could or should help slow Japan's impending economic shrinkage. But the number of physically able and financially independent retirees will surge, and a lot of those individuals will share in the general reawakening to traditional values, including agrarian self-sufficiency.

In France, people frequently take up small-scale cultivation after retirement. They exchange produce and revel in the pleasures of life on the land while enjoying low-cost lifestyles. Most of the late-life farmers will have the chance to experience only a few annual crop cycles, so obtaining sound guidance at the outset is crucial. That guidance is available freely through the volunteerism of experienced farmers and agricultural advisers.

Pastoral sustainability in most nations means large-scale cultivation, corporate agribusiness, and highly integrated regional economies centered on agriculture. Japanese agriculture is struggling for survival by any means, and agrarian opportunities for retirees in the countryside are far from certain. But securing a place for such farmers would certainly help revitalize Japan's withering rural landscape. And making life on the land an economically viable option for young people could transform pastoral Japan dramatically.

Moving to the country is just a single and perhaps far-fetched example of Japan's growing spectrum of lifestyle options. It demonstrates graphically, however, the central issues for Japan in the 21st century:

One, population shrinkage and aging are unavoidable;

Two, they will present daunting challenges;

Three, they will also present unprecedented opportunities for richer, more-fulfilling lifestyles;

Four, fulfilling those opportunities will depend on a thorough reengineering of Japan's socioeconomic systems.

A lot of trial and error will be necessary. Building a social consensus amid the new diversity in values and in modes of work and life will require determined perseverance. Reconciling conflicts of interest will be a huge challenge. But that is all the more reason to get started now. The clock is ticking.

INDEX